d.

house with fully dedicated details | London loft design of
the unexpected but logical | house focussed on perfectly

E

frau und fortschritt I/82

schrift der
Rbge.

erdgas

Hallenbader:
**Alles klar
zum Schwimmen**

Energie:
**Mehr Sowjetgas—
mehr Sicherheit?**

Energiesparen:
**Wärmereserven
in Dämmung
und Heizung**

JEUNE & JOLIE

ADEAU
fiches
es beauté
de couleur
réaliser
esses de l'été

PECIAL
EAUTE
BA
nouveaux
UILLAGES,

40 RAISON
DE SE TROUVE
PLUS BELLE QU
LES COPINE

J'ai 16 an
un cor
de femm
et j'assu

REUSS
SO
HISTOIR
D'AMOU

K KUNSTZEITSCHRIFT

MÄRZ
DM 5

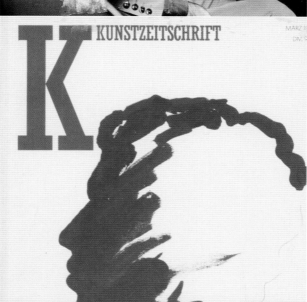

L
Lecturas

525 ptas.
3,16 €

ESPECIAL
MODA

COLECCIONES
PRIMAVERA
VERANO
1999

París
Milán
Barcel
Madri SAARBACH

COLO
Y HUMOR
LA MOD
MÁS DIVERTID

BAÑO
SABROSO

P

a Lobo
servem de inspiração
sical do compositor

ema na
ernet
ução que vai mudar
o filme no mundo

la Camurati
que virou cineasta revela os
s de seu melhor roteiro

ais...
Heitor Cony, Andrucha
gton, poesia sonora,
stello, Cia. do Latão,
de crioula maranhense

DAS COMPAQ MAGAZIN   COMPAQ

8,50 Mark/4,35 EURO | MÄRZ 1/

Web-Orakel
Prognosen bis 2010

Wireless-Art

NO:15

R
ROCK KÜLTÜRÜ DERGISI

W

In your
Face
Clothes That Startle
The Artist Who's
Shocking London

Volume 3 Number 2
$7 USA £5.00

x heigh

The Art Directors' Handbook of Professional Magazine Design

Horst Moser

The Art Directors' Handbook of Professional Magazine Design

Classic Techniques and Inspirational Approaches

Third Edition

CONTENTS

Looking back, magazines are an indispensable source of cultural history, providing a very vivid and compact record of the Zeitgeist. This applies not only to the big names like *Life, Berliner Illustrierte, National Geographic, The New Yorker, Vu, The Economist*, and so on, but also to those relatively short-lived and apparently unimportant magazines in which a valuable and original voice may have been recorded. Great designers have lifted this medium to lofty heights – you've only got to think of names like El Lissitzky, László Moholy-Nagy, Alexey Brodovitch, Alexander Liberman and Willy Fleckhaus. The Dada and Expressionist movements also spawned countless manifesto-type magazines, generally with a very small circulation.

Magazines have changed the world. Einstein's Theory of Relativity, which forms the basis of our world view, first saw the light of day in a magazine. And we mustn't forget the artists and writers who have worked for magazines – Picasso, Warhol, Dalí, Kandinsky, Klee, Matisse, Beardsley, Schwitters, Rodtschenko, Miró, Braque, Chagall, Poe, Schmidt, Tucholsky, Hemingway, Joyce, Kraus, Sartre, the list goes on.

Compared to books, magazine design is more flexible, often more elaborate, more expensive, and more experimental. Photography, typography and illustration all work together. Art directors, like their colleagues in the cinema and theatre – though on far smaller budgets – can create a complete work of art. But in more recent times magazines have had to compete ever more fiercely with other media to gain the public's attention. For a while it even seemed as if the industry was in terminal decline. But after the initial euphoria of the Internet had appeared to herald the death of the printed page, there has been an extraordinary upsurge in the number of highly ambitious magazines – not from the major publishing houses, where the paths of decision-making appear to be too tortuous, but from the smaller firms and the domain of corporate publishing. In the world of science there's now a much more intensive exchange of current ideas. It would be unthinkable for a molecular biologist or an astrophysicist not to be totally up to date with all the latest discoveries.

Some magazines are internationally famous for their editorial design, but there are also many outstanding developments within a narrower, national framework. This book aims to present the very best, state-of-the-art magazine design from all over the world and, by doing so, to provide a fruitful source of ideas. In order to capture the true spirit of contemporary design, I've chosen examples that stem almost exclusively from the new century. Only when dealing with basic themes, or when there are no current examples because other trends have taken over, have I gone back to older specimens.

The book is divided into sections: basic and theoretical issues are followed by practical and technical themes, with the main body devoted to what may be called the grammar of magazine design. The last section presents international treatments of specific subjects, with virtuoso examples of how the basic elements can be applied. As the book had to be kept within manageable proportions, many good examples have unfortunately had to be sacrificed, but perhaps sufficient interest will be generated for further volumes to be published, enabling an even wider range of topics to be embraced.

It's well worth while examining the whole spectrum of magazines published. Before the first edition of a new magazine hits the stands, all those involved are sworn to secrecy. But as soon as the first issue shows its face, it gives away all its own secrets – the format, the typeface, the print, the quality of paper. The whole concept is thrown open to public scrutiny. Even the photographers and illustrators are named in the credits, and everyone can profit from this public revelation.

Every new development may influence international design. These ideas can work on all levels, and their influence doesn't necessarily have to be confined to the obvious highlights. But anyone who merely imitates what they've seen will never be content with the results. Every task has its own particular problems, and so the solutions must always be tailored accordingly.

This book presents a broad spectrum of design and encourages the development of an extensive repertoire, since it's only through a wide range of ideas that the appropriate language of design can consistently be found.

Horst Moser

BRODOVITCH

The foundations of modern magazine design were laid sixty years ago

He worked for twenty-five years as the art director of *Harper's Bazaar*, and during that time he laid the foundations for modern magazine design. This archetypal art director came to New York from Russia, via Paris, and his name was Alexey Brodovitch. If you look at his magazines today, you'll be struck by the fact that even after sixty years the photographers and illustrators are still familiar names: Richard Avedon, Lillian Bassman, Martin Munkácsi, Henri Cartier-Bresson, Erwin Blumenfeld, Man Ray, and Andy Warhol, who made his mark then as a young illustrator with his drawings of shoes. Brodovitch's sureness of touch when it came to choosing quality photographers and illustrators is astonishing. At the time, nearly all of these people were unknown beginners. Just as Griffith, Eisenstein, Chaplin and Hitchcock brought the cinema to a peak, Brodovitch raised his chosen medium to a pinnacle of achievement. Of course there have been new steps forward right through to the present, but never on that scale. There are countless features of outstanding design in the double-page spreads created by this great innovator: his revolutionary use of photographs, asymmetrical layout of pages, three-dimensional effects, breaking the framework of the grid, classic typography, combinations of text and picture, free arrangement of picture material, the design of the unprinted area, rhythmic repetition of pictures, black and white photographs tinted with colour, and so on. His 'Design Laboratory' became a legend, but it was not confined to theory; he was always at pains to get his students to think and act practically and independently, with each one seeking and finding their own way. Nearly three and a half thousand creative talents attended these highly unconventional courses, including such photographers as Irving Penn, Lillian Bassman, and Hiro and Diane Arbus. It was Brodovitch who invested the post of art director with total responsibility for the visual impact of the magazine, and it was he who issued the all-embracing challenge to his colleagues in magazine design: Astonish me!

Harper's Bazaar, November 1935, Photo: Martin Munkácsi

Harper's Bazaar, March 1936, Photo: Man Ray

Harper's Bazaar, March 1950, Photo: Lillian Bassman

Harper's Bazaar, March 1945, Photo: George Hoyningen-Huené

Harper's Bazaar, September 1955, Photo: Richard Avedon

Harper's Bazaar, October 1944, Photo: Martin Munkácsi

Harper's Bazaar, April 1948, Artwork: Henri Matisse

Harper's Bazaar, April 1942, Photo: Erwin Blumenfeld

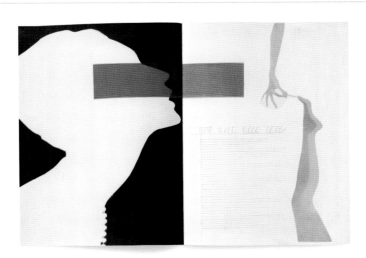

Sketch

Three basic types of magazine art director

Art directors are responsible for the visual elements of a magazine. They can be divided into three basic types: the artistic art director, the virtuoso editorial art director, and a third, special creature that's evolved within the large publishing houses, best identified as an art director whose decisions are all heavily influenced by market research.

Examples of the first category are Neville Brody and David Carson. Their magazine concepts are dominated by their own personal style, and the fact that a magazine is designed by Carson will override all other aspects. This can be an advantage when the designer meets the demand for originality and inventiveness, but of course it can also be a disadvantage.

The second category places emphasis on service, technique, teamwork – this designer is the conductor of an orchestra, bringing out all the essential harmony, counterpoint and rhythms of photography, typography, composition, the blending of black and white with colour, illustrations, charts, and so on. Head and heart have to work together if intellect and emotion are to be correctly balanced, and laws both written and unwritten must be known and observed. What effect do we want to achieve, on whom, and by what means? How can we surprise, provoke, entertain and inform our readers? How can we ensure that our author's text will be read? The virtuoso art director will have mastered a wide variety of design languages and be able to cater for a wide variety of target groups, bringing out all the subtle differences between one concept and another.

With our third category of art director we find the smallest degree of individuality. Their magazines are like the artificial products of chemistry laboratories, emerging from their test-tubes with all the 'right' ingredients. Sometimes these instant packages may even be successful, if your criteria for success are sales figures and income from ads.

Raygun, No. 26, 1995, USA

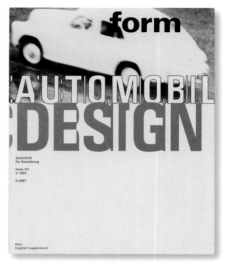

Form, No. 3, 1995, Germany

Neville Brody and David Carson had a huge influence on design in the 1990s. They were prime examples of artistic art directors, and all the magazines they designed carry their own personal touch. They both avoided using normal headline fonts. In some issues of *Raygun* Carson distorted the letters to the point of illegibility, and even sought out weathered inscriptions in public places to inspire a degree of amateurishness in his presentation. Brody designed his own fonts, based on examples from the 1930s and 1940s. His characteristic sign systems enable readers to find their way round his magazines.

Per Lui, February 1990, Italy

Actuel, November 1990, France

Tempo, December 1988/January 1989, Germany

Max, May 1996, Germany

Arena, No. 16, 1989, Great Britain

The Face, No. 69, 1986, Great Britain

11

SKETCHING

The precondition for good design is conceptual thinking

One of the attractions of the computer screen is that whatever you put on it will somehow look good. It's also easy to try out countless variations, shifting your images back and forth, making them bigger, making them smaller – it's all really helpful. Or is it? There's a danger that you'll be tempted to begin without knowing exactly where you want to go. Of course, it's not easy to just force yourself to start sketching, and you do normally have some idea of what you're aiming at. But it's far better and far less time-consuming to have a precise concept. First of all, read the text that's to be designed. Then consider the visual elements that are available or that will have to be devised. For instance, if you're dealing with a report that's already accompanied by photographs, you'll have to make a careful selection: which pictures should you put first, are there others that follow on logically, how will these others be grouped, do the colours go together, is the sequence too repetitive, does it add something new to what we already know? If the overall design leaves you freedom of choice regarding the font, which one do you choose, and why? For the sake of everyone who works on the magazine there should be good reasons for this choice, which must also be practical. If it's merely a matter of personal taste, then the decision-making process becomes arbitrary and even arrogant.

The designer is also usually the first reader of the article, and may feel that there are questions to be asked about one aspect or another; these may find their way into a box or a margin in the form of additional information. The designer must have a total grasp of the content if they're to work in partnership with the editor, and if together they're to find the optimum form of presentation. Supposing, for instance, the text is too long-winded, the designer should suggest ways of dividing it up into palatable sections. Or if a factual description is not clear enough, the designer has to devise other means of animating the presentation.

Peter Knapp, former art director of the French magazine *Elle*, drew designs for most of his magazines and books on large sketch pads. This is the best way to get a feeling for the rhythm of a section, or indeed of a whole issue.

There are many different views on what constitutes the perfect sequence of subjects or the rhythm of a magazine as it emerges during the compilation and structural planning of the material. The classic form is quite like that of a grand opera. You whet the appetite with the overture, which offers a short introduction to all the main themes – the magazine equivalent being the editorial and the list of contents. Next the opera may introduce us to shorter passages and fragments of melodies, building up to the climax of a great aria – here the magazine equivalent is a sequence of short announcements or articles, before embarking on the major theme. There are, of course, many possible variations on this structure. The editor of the German edition of *Wiener* came up with the idea of beginning a red-hot feature on page two – even before the editorial and contents – and stretching it over several pages in order to grab the reader's attention straight away, like a front door opening straight into a living-room. Fashion magazines tend to begin with a big block of ads, with the main bulk of editorial material found later on. You could argue that many readers don't actually read from beginning to end, but open up at random or even flick through backwards, and this is definitely true. Even so, the structure should be as logical and comprehensible as possible, so that even the casual browser is aware of what they're disregarding.

In order to explain their own principles of design and methods of composition, many designers compare their work to other fields. Brody, for instance, refers to examples from architecture, and says that he tried to base his design for *The Face* on town planning, guiding his reader through the magazine with signposts and, at particular points, with open spaces. These are always at the beginning of a piece, where the white space is used to denote the entrance. If you have a large building, he argues, you're not going to place its entrance down a little alley.

Alexey Brodovitch compared his double-page spreads in *Harper's Bazaar* to film sequences, and used the term 'flow' to describe the narrative and rhythmic qualities of his designs. He would lay all the pages in their original size out on the floor, and then shuffle and juxtapose them until he'd established the best order.

Willy Fleckhaus used the image of a well-stocked table, a buffet from which readers could serve themselves. In particular he visualized it as Italian cuisine – the art of the simple. The basic menu of hors d'oeuvre, main dish, and dessert is certainly appropriate for the layout of many magazines.

Peter Knapp, sketches

LAYOUT VARIATIONS

A secret competition between Neville Brody's *The Face* and Lo Breier's *Wiener*

THEORETICAL FOUNDATIONS

The vast number of possible variations in magazine design is not self-evident from the finished products. The publishing firms and design studios may try out lots of things, but most of the results remain hidden from the public. Nevertheless, every variation in design gives a different slant to the actual material, changing the appearance – and message – of any given article to a greater or lesser extent. The choice of opening picture sets the mood for the rest, and the typography has a decisive influence on this mood. An exemplary case from 1983 illustrates these influences perfectly: eight European magazines – *Actuel, Wiener, The Face, Oor, El Vibora, Frigidaire, ETC,* and *Tip* – got together on a joint project with the theme of Europe. For their November editions all eight tackled the same subjects, with each editorial board making its own contributions. They all worked with the same material, though not all the contributions were printed in every magazine. Some themes, though, were published in several magazines, and it's through these that you can compare the different presentations. In some cases, top quality art directors were at work, and so there are very clear differences in standards. Taking the story about Boy George for example, *Tip* opens with a typical, garish publicity photo accompanied by deadly dull typography, while *Wiener* opens with a large black and white picture that promises a personal and exclusive story. In any article on pop stars, the promise of exclusive revelations inevitably arouses far more curiosity than the usual PR material. The interviewer asks his questions on behalf of the reader, and the more original and probing these questions are, the closer the reader feels to the star concerned. In this respect, the design has a very positive effect. Even though it cannot influence the actual text, it can certainly effect the atmosphere and the impact. In *The Face*, Brody uses a similar picture to the one used in *Tip*, but the accompanying typography makes all the difference. It creates a completely modern mood, arousing interest in the story itself.

Another theme from this Europe project offers a pot-pourri of new ideas from all areas of culture. While the choice of different artists naturally gave each issue its own special character, they all used the same cover photo, taken by the Austrian photographer Margit Marnul: a child in jeans. Here too we can see very clearly how the context, logo and typography can influence the overall impact of the photograph. A similar experiment took place in 1999, though on a smaller scale: the different provincial editions of *Max* agreed to combine operations, but since they were already very similar in their overall concepts, the differences turned out to be far less striking.

Tip, No. 23, 1983, Germany

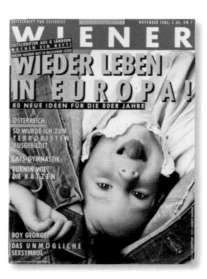

Wiener, No. 11, 1983, Austria

The Face, No. 43, 1983, Great Britain

Tip, No. 23, 1983, Germany

In 1983, eight contemporary magazines got together on a joint project. For their Europe edition, each editorial board thought up themes relating to their own country but also connected in some way with Europe. The texts were identical, but the layout of each magazine – sometimes using the same pictures – was done independently. The differences demonstrate the wide variety of possible forms of expression through design.

Wiener, No. 11, 1983, Austria

The Face, No. 43, 1983, Great Britain

The Face, No. 43, 1983, Great Britain

Wiener, No. 11, 1983, Austria

EDITORIAL COOPERATION

The role of the art director in the editing process

The first step for every issue of a magazine is a conference on subject matter. Here the lines are laid down for the whole issue, with editors and heads of department putting their proposals to the board, who discuss and decide. It's important for the various creative talents involved to take part in this first phase of the process. Their ideas can have a powerful influence on the direction an individual article will take, as well as on the final stages of planning once the themes have been selected from the different proposals. But it's especially in the overall composition of the magazine that the visual aspect will be of vital importance.

At the next conference, individual contributions are discussed and visual ideas formulated. In addition to the senior editor, the authors of the different articles (or the editors responsible) and the art directors and picture editors should also take part. Unfortunately at this stage there are very rarely any completed texts available – only bare summaries. It would, of course, be ideal if the texts were already finished, as the language and the atmosphere they create can themselves inspire visual conceptualizations. The more fragmentary the text, the more general and vague the pictorial concept will be. With many editorial boards these conferences can place an intolerable burden on the art directors, who are expected to come up with a whole range of spontaneous ideas there and then. Creativity needs time. For this reason, most proposals made at such meetings relate to pictures that are already in existence, although it should be the ambition of every editorial team to create something new, or to reveal something that has never been seen before.

'The future of the art director' – a conversation between Horst Moser and Mike Meiré

HM: Magazine design is very similar to other phenomena like fashion and furniture design – one revival takes the place of another. Way back in the 1940s a magazine genius like Brodovitch solved a vast number of design problems for ever. Why are there now fewer and fewer formal innovations?

MM: I don't find it at all frustrating that everything's already been done. In fact ultimately I see it as a kind of liberation, because it enables me to concentrate on more fundamental things. The art director is evolving more and more into a sort of producer, who brings together various disciplines and areas of design. When all is said and done, we magazine-makers are the creators of new desires or even perhaps of new forms of consciousness, and as I see it, this is a very different and much more complex challenge. I don't regard myself as an art director or designer in the conventional sense. What interests me isn't the question of formal innovation but the need to realize that we must get to grips with our own identity, and I think that will have an influence on the future design of magazines. As a designer, you can channel and inspire people, like a theatre director, but then you're no longer just a designer who's presented with texts and photos that he's supposed to make something beautiful out of. Incidentally, in Paris there's an agency where you can hire art directors just like photographers and models. This means that the art director is taking up an ever more important position in the whole chain of information processing, and of course that heightens the profile and makes the job more demanding – which I think is an exciting development.

HM: Of course this development requires the exact opposite of your ordinary graphic designer, who sets the text as greyscale.

MM: That's something which imposes its own limitations. It seems to me at the moment that there's a development towards deceleration, a slowing down that's not trying to suppress complexity – that's something that can't be done, it would be stupid, a step backwards – but we need to settle the media disciplines, calm them down. But I could just as easily imagine that there'll be a counter movement to promote cross cultures and bring about an increase in complexity. That would lead to a sort of collage, pictures being stuck onto or fading into one another. Pictures seen as different levels of information, interwoven with texts, so that spaces and depths arise on the paper, where everything is blended together. You could almost talk of communication architects.

HM: In between floods of hectic innovation there have always been quiet patches, where innovation – in design too – has been seen as completely unnecessary or even absurd. For instance, in medieval icon painting. The master would pass on all his knowledge to his pupil who would use it in precisely the same way as his predecessors. No one thought of expressing himself in his own way, and diverging from the paths of tradition. In the Egyptian Museum in Cairo you can see sandals whose design hasn't varied for the last three thousand years. Even in really fashion-conscious fields like hairstyles there are classics that don't change – like the Julius Caesar style.

MM: Archetypes are always being produced, and I could imagine creating a classic magazine even now. But that doesn't mean that I'm an out-and-out classical man. I can surf the Internet, and zap between three hundred programmes, though at the same time I like to sit in front of a fire on a winter's night and drink a glass of mulled wine and maybe read a good magazine. That's not a contradiction – I think there's something nice about that.

HM: The idea of deceleration of course runs counter to the credo of many magazine makers, who think you should always strive to be topical.

MM: Even a weekly magazine can never really be bang up to date, and of course that's even more true of monthlies. As far as quarterlies are concerned, the question of topicality never even arises. If I want information on current affairs, I turn to the daily newspaper, the TV or the Internet.

HM: What functions will be left for magazines to perform in the future?

MM: I think you can only keep trying to create a forum, or communicate identities and attitudes that will run right through the magazine. I imagine that there'll be a lot more special interest magazines in the future, filling particular niches.

HM: The business magazine *Brand eins* has dispensed with all the conventional measuring devices like charts and tables, and compared to what the normal reader would expect, the texts are very long.

MM: The craze for only allowing short snippets, as apparently we're no longer able to read long sentences, means that ideas discussed in interviews get badly rehashed, because we have to reduce them to extracts that simply can't reproduce the full substance of what's actually been said. I can't accept that in a world that's become increasingly complex, we're supposed to pretend that it can all be described in three words. With *Brand eins* I only want to see text, because at the moment I'm not interested in the form but in the content. I know that these new subjects or new ideas will also give rise to new patterns on the formal level. I'm a designer who designs content – and there the first priority is the word. The content is the word, and the word is the content – full stop. And if people don't want to read it, because maybe it's too long for them... well, OK, there's plenty of other things to do. I don't have to please everybody.

GRID SYSTEMS

The number and width of columns influence the character of a magazine

The right layout of columns is immensely important for the structure of a magazine page. How many columns there are depends on the format and on the length of the lines, which should contain approximately sixty characters each for optimal readability. But there are many factors at work here. First of all, the choice of font and the space between the letters. Coloured lettering has a different effect from black, and the leading also makes a difference. Of course you need to know the rules, but in the end, after you've tried out the various settings, sizes and spacings, you'll have to decide for yourself which combination is the easiest to read. Another important factor is the paper you intend to use: matt and glossy surfaces affect readability in different ways.

Apart from these material considerations, the content also influences the choice of layout. If, for instance, you know that a particular section is going to contain a lot of addresses, you'll need to ensure that the column is wide enough to prevent awkward breaks. Another important element is the format of your ads. Very few magazines only allow full- or double-page ads; those which take up half, two-thirds, or three-quarters of the page require different column divisions. A vertical, half-page ad will need a two- or four-column grid, whereas an ad that occupies two-thirds of the page can only be accommodated in a three-column layout. The four-column system has certain disadvantages (the shortness of the lines, for instance, and a tendency

towards quite a monotonous symmetry) and so a mixture of grids within the magazine is advisable. The choice, though, naturally needs to fit in with the content. Sections containing long texts can be divided into two or three columns and the appropriate ads can be inserted in those pages. Small sections can use the four-column system, and can incorporate half-page and quarter-page ads. A well-composed page can also allow for marginal columns. Originally, this narrow border was used for snippets of text, but in modern magazines it now accommodates small pictures, captions, quotations, and illustrations that overshoot the width of the column. The wandering margin is a special form, and this narrow column frequently changes its position, facilitating a rich variety of page layouts.

In some magazines the column widths are completely irregular – *Leica World*, for instance. In this magazine, it's impossible to shorten or lengthen the text of the exclusive interviews, and so the only corrective is the length and breadth of the columns. When a system changes within a single text, the impact of that text also changes. In some cases, the layout of the opening double-page spread may differ from that of the pages that follow, and clever variation of these grid systems can influence the whole character of a magazine: it may appear pleasantly calm and relaxed, or it may generate a feeling of pace and excitement. Both have their uses, but of course it's vital that the choice isn't arbitrary. The system must always fit in with the nature of the content.

Esquire, March 2002, Great Britain, flexible margins

In the magazine *Leica World* there's no fixed grid because it's impossible to change the length of the exclusive interviews. The width and number of columns therefore depends on the amount of text.

Leica World, No. 1, 2000, Germany

Leica World, No. 1, 1998, Germany

Leica World, No. 1, 1998, Germany

Leica World, No. 2, 1997, Germany

Leica World, No. 2, 2000, Germany

Leica World, No. 2, 2000, Germany

Mini International, No. 1, 2001, Germany

1/4 nach 5, No. 5, 2002, Germany

Lucky, No. 9, 2001, USA

Jalouse, November 2001, France

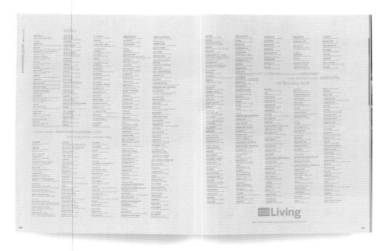

Martha Stewart Living, March 2002, USA (see index for credits)

Esquire, March 2002, Great Britain

Soda, No. 17, 2001, Switzerland

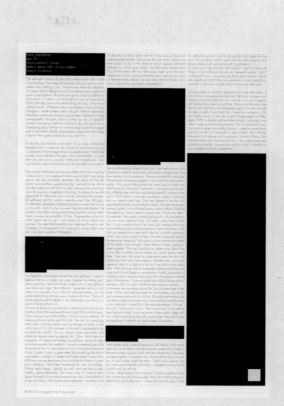

RE, No. 3, 1998, Netherlands

Frame, No. 19, 2001, Netherlands

Artist, No. 1, 2002, Germany

How rigid or flexible should the instructions be?

As soon as the concept of a magazine has been settled, the composition of sample pages or of a design manual follows. It's always important to bear in mind who's subsequently going to be responsible for the layout. Sometimes the proprietor will leave the actual compilation of the magazine to people who have no training in design, and in such cases provision has to be made within the original concept for a correspondingly straightforward layout. When the staff don't have specialist knowledge of magazine design, it's a good idea to set out all the desired variations on the sample pages, and to give precise definitions of any exceptions. But this would be inappropriate for magazines that are produced by experts, since too much regulation removes the vital element of surprise and results in monotony. In all cases, you have to allow for the working methods of those responsible for the layout. Should everything be defined by way of existing stylistic models, or should only the most important elements be preserved? There are always going to be different solutions to every problem, but even when detailed instructions are necessary, you should always bear in mind that too much information can actually be a hindrance.

When can the sample pages be regarded as finished with? Definitions must first be tested in practice, and two or three issues are generally needed before the process of development can be seen as complete. There may still be elements that need modification or extension, and it's important that the experiences and suggestions of those who work daily with these sample pages are taken into account.

Unfortunately, most firms have now dispensed with the printing of manuals, and the sample pages are generally only available in digital form. One example, though, that was not only a manual but was also intended as a book of ideas for designers, was published in 1992 for the German edition of the magazine *Forbes*.

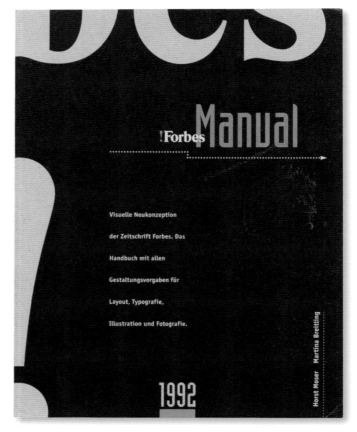

!Forbes Manual

Visuelle Neukonzeption der Zeitschrift Forbes. Das Handbuch mit allen Gestaltungsvorgaben für Layout, Typografie, Illustration und Fotografie.

1992

Horst Moser Martina Breitling

Forbes Manual, 1992, Germany, cover and inside pages (right)

FORMATS

Different factors to be considered in the choice of format

If you're starting up a new magazine, you'll soon be confronted with the problem of the format. Your choice will be influenced by a number of different factors: when and where will the magazine be read? Plane, train, café, underground, study or living room? Does it need to fit into a handbag or briefcase? If it's to be distributed by post, will it need a special-sized envelope? How important will the ads be? Will you need to take into account the clients' existing advertising format so that you don't lose them? What will be the impact of the format when the magazine is opened? Is it nice to handle? The content will also influence the format. If, for example, every edition is to contain thirty recipes, with each dish being photographed on a round plate, the best format will be more or less square. If there are going to be lots of oblong photos of snowboarders, you don't want a narrow, vertical format. The basic format of *Leica World*, for example, is that of the 35 mm photograph, and so a vertical picture suitably enlarged covers the entire page. As the magazine has glued binding, there's always a narrow unprinted strip – the gutter – so that no detail of the picture will be lost.

The format and the paper, as well as the strength of the paper (g/m^2), are all interdependent, and so before embarking on production, it's worth while creating a dummy. This will enable you to test whether the paper and its strength go together with the format and the thickness planned, and whether the magazine will be too rigid or too floppy. Even the relative strengths of the cover and the inside pages can be important for the overall feel. The German magazine *Max* has a very thin cover which can easily be torn off the staples. The same is true of the American editions of *Rolling Stone* and *Interview*. There are also issues relating to printing technology: does the chosen format fit in with the formats normally created by the paper manufacturer? Which printing press would be the most economical to use for the quantities required? Inappropriate formats can very quickly lead to spiralling costs. In other words, with close attention to the correct use of technology, and with sometimes very minor adjustments, you can often make far better use of paper and machinery and avoid unnecessary expense.

Mare has a standard format of 21 × 28 cm, while *Glamour's* 'handbag' format suits the mobility of its target group. *The Manipulator*, at 49.5 × 70 cm, is the largest magazine so far to appear on the market.

Mare, No. 25, 2001, Germany, 21 × 28 cm (8¼ × 11 in.)

Glamour, October 2001, Italy, 17 × 22.5 cm (6¾ × 8¾ in.)

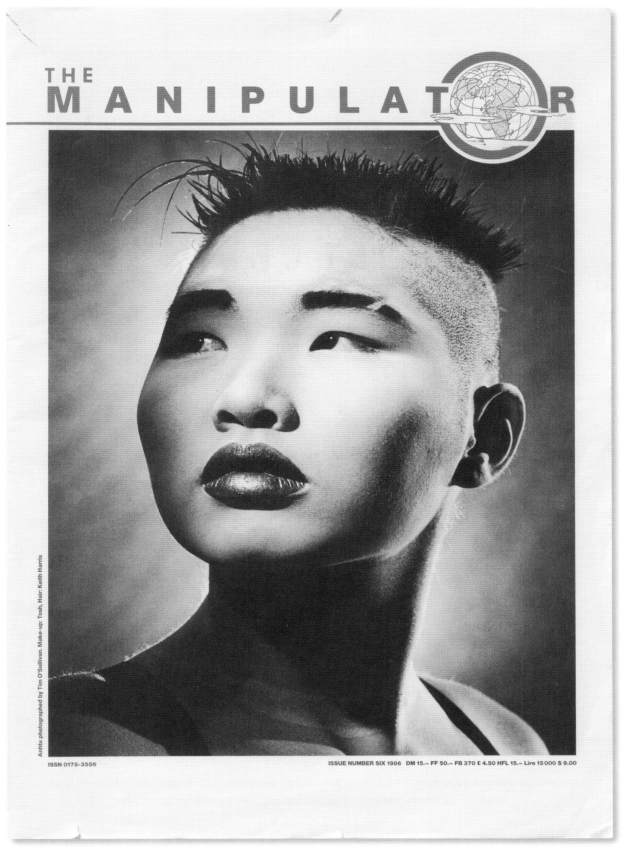

The Manipulator, June 1986, Germany, 49.5 × 70 cm (19½ × 27⅝ in.)

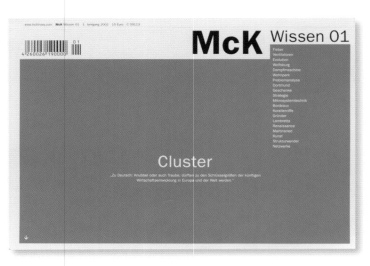

McK Wissen, No. 1, 2002, Germany, 28 × 19.5 cm (11 × 7⅝ in.)

Double, Winter 2006, France, 29.7 x 23 cm (11⅝ x 9 in.)

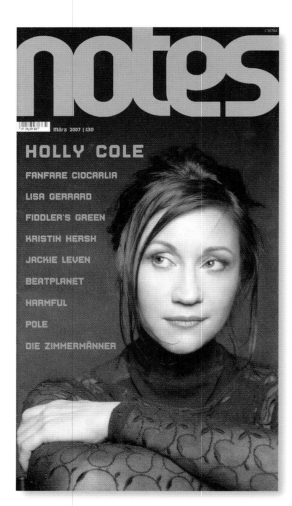

Notes, March 2007, Germany, 16.3 x 30 cm (6⅜ x 11¾ in.)

Room, April – July 2002, Germany, 27 × 28 cm (10⅝ × 11 in.)

Re-Magazine, Winter/Spring 2004, Netherlands, 20.6 x 28.8 cm (8⅛ x 11¼ in.)

Matador, Vol.D, 1999, Spain, 30 × 40 cm (11¾ × 15¾ in.)

A new feel to the pages: instead of turning them from right to left, you turn them from bottom to top in *McK Wissen*. *Re-Magazine* uses a 'widescreen' format that is then folded again, while *Double* combines landscape and portrait elements. There are no limits to the range of shapes and sizes: they may be tall and slim like *Notes*, virtually square like *Room*, or an oversized classic rectangle like *Matador*.

REFINEMENTS

Cut-outs, indentations, gloss, holograms and picture puzzles

There's a virtually infinite variety of effects that can be used to attract attention in the marketplace, and to distinguish your product from the opposition. They're only available, though, to high-priced magazines with lofty aesthetic ambitions, because the more outlandish the special effect, the more expensive it will be to produce. Even so, current trends suggest that for the sake of originality, this is a risk that's frequently being taken.

One method of getting your magazine to stand out from the crowd is to use cut-outs. *Flaunt* makes particularly creative use of this device. There may be gaps in the page through which you catch a glimpse of a woman's face, or you may be invited to open a window. They keep coming up with new variations that add new twists to this game of visual hide and seek. But the cut-outs are limited to the cover and front page, and the rectangular format of the magazine remains conventional. This is not so with the magazine *Nest*, which uses a completely new shape, the normal rectangular edge of the pages being broken up by irregular curves. The rounded corners of *Designers Digest* seem relatively conservative by comparison; the designer, Marko Thiele, adapted this outline to fit in with his playful typographical experiments.

Other popular devices are reflective surfaces, holograms, transparent paper, indentations and gloss. These special effects are strengthened if they actually coincide with and complement a particular idea. A classic example of this was the cover of *Das Büro* that was made from a piece of carpet. This would certainly have elicited the desired 'Wow!' from its readers – but such successes are the exception rather than the rule. Effects for their own sake may be striking at first glance, but they make no lasting impact. In one edition of *Visionaire*, Stephen Gan used a picture puzzle that revealed a different picture depending on the way you held it up. In this case the effect corresponded perfectly with the subject: supermodel Kate Moss sitting on a swing whose movement was recreated by moving the picture. Transparent or glossy materials are less expensive than some other refinements, and a wide variety of interesting aesthetic effects can be created through the interplay of dull and shiny.

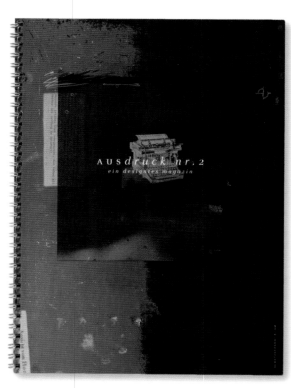

Ausdruck, No. 2, 1997, Germany

Brett, No. 8, 2000, Germany

RE, No. 23, 1997, Netherlands

Tank, Best of Tank Magazine 1998 – 2000, Great Britain

Apart from conventional staple and glue bindings, there are
various ways of holding the pages together: a simple spiral
binding (*Ausdruck*), a single screw (*Brett*), string or rivets
(*Form+Zweck*), or an elastic band (*RE*). In 2002 a collection of
the Best of Tank appeared in the form of a cigarette packet.

Form+Zweck, No. 6, 1992, Germany

Form+Zweck, No. 11, 1995, Germany

The whole magazine may be rounded off at the edges (*Designers Digest* and *Nest*), or just the cover may be perforated, punched or cut out, as in the peekaboo style of *Flaunt*.

Designers Digest, No. 77, 2001, Germany

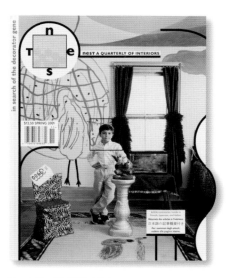

Nest, No. 12, 2001, USA

Nest, No. 16, 2002, USA

Flaunt, May 1999, USA

Flaunt, September 2001, USA

Flaunt, June/July 1999, USA

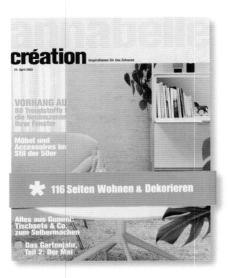

Annabelle Création, April 2002, Switzerland

Another Magazine, No. 2, 2002, Great Britain

Ecuad, 1999/2000, Singapore

Rosebud, No. 2, 2001, Germany

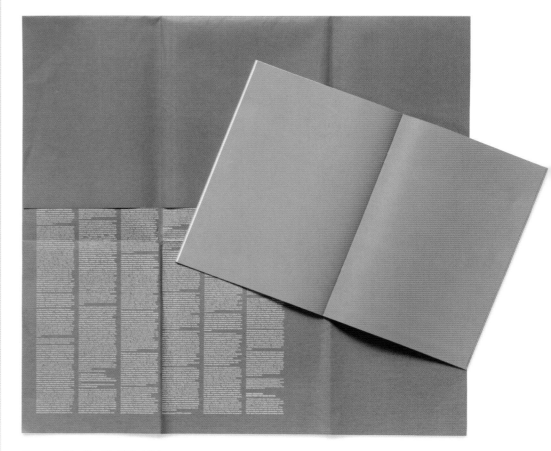

Typographic, No. 58, 2002, USA

If you want to attract attention in the marketplace, you need to come up with new ideas: a simple paper band draws the eye to *Annabelle Création*; a purple lace bookmark does the same for *Another Magazine*; Singapore's *Ecuad* has a transparent cover; the US magazine *Typographic* is in the form of a poster; *Rosebud* is wrapped in silver foil.

Visionaire, No. 29, 1999, USA

Visionaire, No. 28, 1999, USA

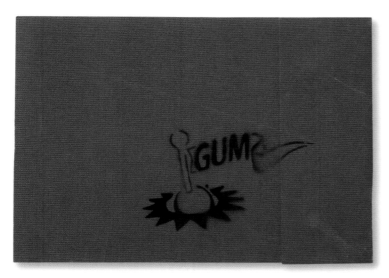

Gum, No. 5, 1999, Germany

Das Büro 1, No. 10, 1996, Germany

Tactile magazines: rough felt (*Das Büro*);
fine silk (*Visionaire*); sandpaper (*Gum*);
indentations and gilt edging (*Visionaire*).

Visionaire, No. 4232, USA

Jalouse, May 2000, France

Kate Moss on a swing in *Visionaire*, and an ad for the Chanel perfume 'Allure' in *Jalouse* –
two effective attention-grabbers.

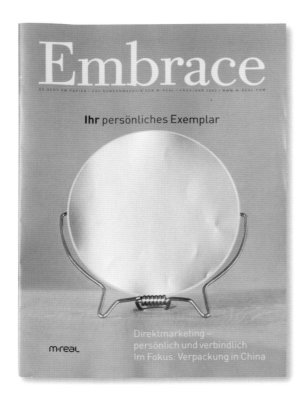

Embrace, No. 1, 2002, Finland

Vogue, December 1999, Great Britain

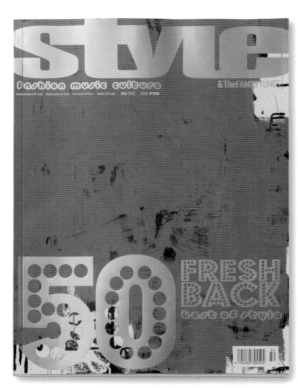

Style, No. 50, 2002, Germany

Domus, No. 788, 1996, Italy

The trend for reflective surfaces: partial, as with the mirror in *Embrace*; total, with the rich silver of *Vogue*; iridescent in *Domus*; a bronze effect in *Style*.

THE AVENUE BOX

A magazine becomes a box of surprises

Magazines are not read like novels, from beginning to end. People tend to leaf through, and they start reading when their eye alights on something that catches their attention. That is, assuming you *can* leaf through. It's not always easy. In a lot of fashion and design magazines, there are so many samples, inserts and supplements that you just keep getting stuck in the same places. Many readers help themselves out by getting rid of all the intruders before they even start reading, but there's an interesting alternative to the stuffing technique: the Dutch magazine *Avenue* launched itself onto the market as a box. The box contained the magazine, together with the whole collection of samples and supplements. A great idea, since it allows the advertiser to promote his products without obstructing the reader's access to the magazine itself. Still, from the point of view of cost and handling, this form isn't without its problems.

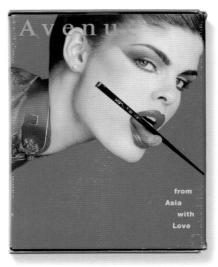

Avenue, No. 1, 1994, Netherlands

Avenue, No. 4, 1994, Netherlands

Avenue, No. 3, 1995, Netherlands

Avenue, No. 5, 1994, Netherlands

Avenue, No. 1, 1995, Netherlands

Avenue, No. 3, 1994, Netherlands

Avenue, No. 5, 1995, Netherlands

Avenue, No. 6, 1995, Netherlands

Avenue, No. 2, 1995, Netherlands

Avenue, No. 2, 1994, Netherlands

PICTURE FRAMES

From the work of art to games with frames

A lot of people don't even think of picture-framing as an aspect of design, and when it comes to layout, all too often no consideration is given to how an illustration is to be enclosed. It seems to be taken for granted that photos will be cut into rectangles without borders. But different forms of enclosure can create striking effects. Ideally, there should be a link between the picture and its frame. One of the commonest devices is the irregular border that surrounds enlarged photos, and this serves to emphasize the aesthetic craftsmanship of the photographer's art. It also suggests a certain stylistic

level which would not be appropriate for, say, a football report. The conventional photo frame is redolent of the museum or gallery, where framed paintings hang at some distance from each other in order to avoid any sort of distraction. This enables them to live their own lives. In magazines, the decision on whether to bleed pictures or provide them with identical frames will have a major influence on how they are perceived. In the one case, the result will be an increased dynamism; in the other, uniformity will tend to create more detachment.

Harper's Bazaar, July 1994, USA

Rails, July/August 2000, Netherlands

P, No. 17, 1999, Germany/Great Britain

Rails, March 2001, Netherlands

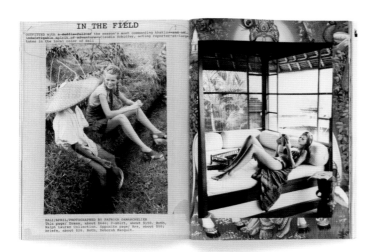

Harper's Bazaar, April 1994, USA

Harper's Bazaar, April 1994, USA

Rails, No. 4, 2001, Netherlands

Harper's Bazaar, April 1994, USA

Harper's Bazaar, February 1996, USA

NRC Handelsblad, April 2001, Netherlands

VISUAL METASYSTEMS

When there's a spontaneous overview, reading plays a secondary role

A well-thought-out magazine has an identity of its own. It's distinguished from other magazines by certain special qualities both of written content and of visual presentation – the texts and the design. The first impression, of course, will be made by the cover, which combines the different elements of logo, picture and typography in such a way as to create a totally individual and unmistakable identity. This image must be coherent and consistent to guarantee repeated recognition in the marketplace. If every edition were to look different, the reader wouldn't have any precise image in mind: a memorable appearance distinct from all the opposition is integral to commercial success. Still, it must be said that very few magazines could be safely identified if the title were covered up.

The extent of information that can be conveyed by the metasystems becomes clear if we experiment with a blurred, unreadable page from a newspaper. The moment we look at this page, the typographical system already gives us a feeling of familiarity. By a process of visual elimination, we can easily establish what kind of page it is not: we can see that it's not a cover, a collection of facts and figures from the financial pages, an illustrated report, or part of the arts section. Sport would also look quite different. Once you've eliminated all the rest, you're left with the classified section, and in particular recruitment. There's no doubt about this, and you can even say with a degree of certainty what kind of jobs are being advertised. They're not for high fliers, and even ads for middle management would be in a different format. Anyone really familiar with this type of recruitment ad would probably even be able to recognize individual firms. And yet we've not been able to read a single letter. If we'd not learned these formal systems, we'd never be able to skim through the pages of magazines, to select or ignore particular sections. If you were now to imagine the ads on this page presented as continuous text, without distinction, set in the same font and the same size, you would get some idea of the time and effort that goes into the typography of such a

section, regardless of its quality. With any magazine that we know or recognize, we can name the components that give it a particular character. In this context, covers with some overall concept are the easiest to analyse. The less precise the concept, or the more flexible and variable the design, the more difficult it will be to identify the magazine. Every designer has to be aware of the rules that govern the overall image, and this should be part of their basic training. When it comes to a new concept, or to redesigning an old one, the extent to which these rules should be applied or broken will then, of course, be up to them, but either way, the process can only work if the designer is fully conscious of what they're doing. The Swiss designer Hans-Rudolf Lutz gave an extraordinary demonstration of this in 1977, when he experimented with the covers of the magazine *Typografische Monatsblätter*. When you see the covers, you think they belong to other, well-known magazines. Only when you look and read more closely do you realize that you've been misled: the letters give the name 'Typografische Monatsblätter', but the strikingly familiar visual components of the other magazines – typography, logos, colours and pictures – suggest a different identity. This demonstrates that our first impression is through general perception rather than through reading. The reverse of this experiment can be seen from the aftermath of Princess Diana's death: her picture appeared on countless magazine covers, and although she was one of the most photographed people of all time, there were not so many photos available at that particular moment for every journal to use a different one. As a result, many of the covers contained the same picture, and this uniformity unquestionably meant that each magazine had to sacrifice a degree of its own identity. At first sight it's extremely difficult to make any distinction between them. A closer inspection, though, reveals interesting differences in the typography and other minor details. In some cases, the black and white photo has been coloured to give it greater popular appeal.

Typografische Monatsblätter, May 1977, Switzerland

Typografische Monatsblätter, June/July 1977, Switzerland

Typografische Monatsblätter, December 1977, Switzerland

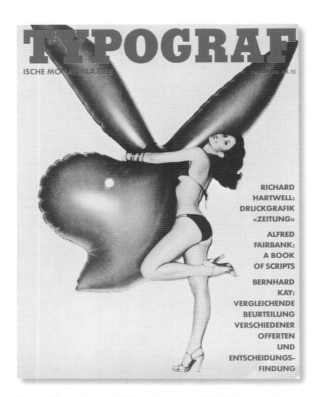

Typografische Monatsblätter, December 1977, Switzerland

First impressions may deceive: 1970s editions of
Typografische Monatsblätter imitated the covers of
other well-known magazines.

Who, September 1997, Australia

People, September 1997, Great Britain

Gioia, September 1997, Italy

Stern, September 1997, Germany

Nokta, September 1997, Turkey

Point De Vue, August 1998, France

Intimità, September 1998, Italy

Facts, September 1997, Switzerland

Neue Revue, September 1997, Germany

Visual metasystems function only through an individual pictorial language. With global media events like the death of Princess Diana, the use of the same pictures cancels out individual identities. It's interesting that even though the same photo is on every cover, there are still many variations possible through size and position, background, reversal, colour, and so on. The different effects of the typography on the picture are also very clear.

The role of the avant-garde in magazine design

Not many people would ask why *Time* magazine looks completely different from, say, *Die Gartenlaube* – and that's a pity. The power of innovation is vital to the very existence of magazines. There's about a hundred-year gap between *Die Gartenlaube* and *Time*, and both are deeply rooted in their own period, totally mainstream and anything but avant-garde. But their covers could not be more different. *Die Gartenlaube* is rather like one of those late nineteenth-century, stucco-ceilinged old houses, rampant with the eclectic ornamentation typical of the period. *Time* has a single, full-page picture, and a classical logotype, with all the normative power of the tried and tested. While the differences between the covers are very marked, those on the inside are only minor. The layout of the columns and the positioning of the illustrations are structurally quite similar, and considering the vast array of artistic 'isms' that separate the two – Impressionism, Expressionism, Cubism, Dadism, Futurism, the Bauhaus and New Functionalism, Art Nouveau, Art Deco, Art Informel, Tachisme, Pop Art and all its derivatives – remarkably little has changed.

When and where do innovations – even if not particularly radical ones in this case – actually spring from, and who initiates them? Looking at the current situation, the fact is that every new initiative by the big publishing firms is under the shadow of a 'me too' mentality, with any trace of innovation being wiped out by the germ-killers of market research. Anyone involved in the development of magazines will have experienced this painful process, and if they have a dozen designers on the payroll, any revolutionary proposal will need to be modified with an evolutionary sweetener. This trend is reflected in the vast majority of magazines found on sale at the news-stand. And quite apart from the cold-feet mentality of most proprietors, the tiny budget allocated to development means that there's neither time nor resources available for the sort of visual research that might produce practicable innovations. The task of promoting the new falls to those magazines that exist within more independent structures. They are free from the 'that's how we've always done it' syndrome, and thanks to their short and swift decision-making processes, which are not always based on the lowest common denominator, they're the ones who are able to charge their printing presses with the unconventional. And from the work of these magazines, which act as a kind of research laboratory, the big publishing houses then proceed to profit.

Die Gartenlaube (illustrated family journal), 1897, Germany

Die Gartenlaube (illustrated family journal), 1897, Germany

Time, May 2000, USA

Time, March 1991, USA

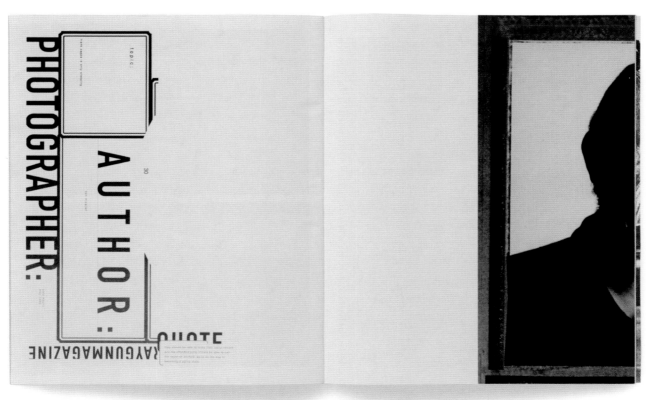

Raygun, No. 10, 1995, USA

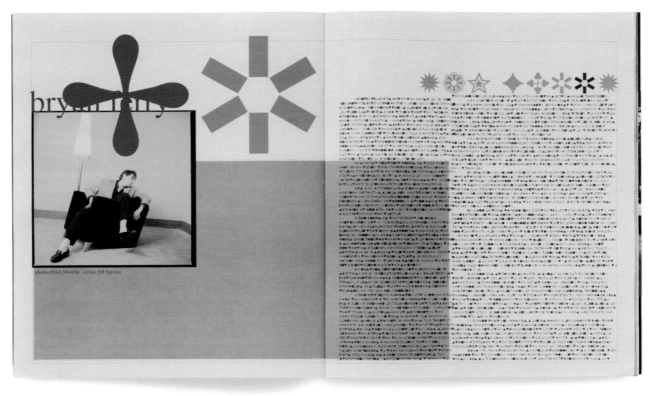

Raygun, No. 11, 1994, USA

INTRODUCTION TO COVER DESIGN

A balancing act between surprise and familiarity

The cover is crucial to the success of any magazine and must encapsulate its whole character. Virtually every genre has developed its own forms, which of course are heavily dependent on the tastes of the time: covers of top contemporary fashion magazines, for instance, mostly offer a very narrow range of variations on the portrait theme. Even the form of these portraits is usually very similar: faces in close-up, head and shoulders, or half-length. Eye contact is almost universal, although this has always been pretty general and is not a specifically modern trait. Though if you look at the covers of *Harper's Bazaar* or *Vogue* from the 1930s or 1940s, you're struck by the extraordinary variety and inventiveness of the ideas.

Computer magazines have developed their own aesthetics to which the majority conform. Once again, there's a 'me too' mentality instead of any attempt to create an original, independent brand that will distinguish itself from the opposition.

On the other hand, the covers of some business magazines are astonishingly unconventional. *Fast Company, Quote, Red Herring* and *Business 2.0* have all come up with highly distinctive designs that leave the old norms far behind. *Fortune* was the progenitor of this breed, and during the first few decades of its existence came up with quite outstanding covers. Since then its quality has plummeted.

If you try to call magazine covers to mind, the memorable ones are those that offer a powerful image or striking individuality. They're the ones your eyes alight on, and of course that's their purpose – the one means they have of shining forth from the news-stand. Of the thousands of covers we see, though, the vast majority will be instantly forgettable. This is of little importance to subscribers, who receive their favourites through the post and are therefore no longer spoilt for choice, but what's the secret of the attention-grabbers? Certainly not the 'me too' principle. Brodovitch's challenge of the 1930s and 1940s is just as valid today as it was then: astonish me! Astonishment, though, should not degenerate into shock.

Whoever buys a magazine expects to find something new in it. The cover must also be new, but at the same time, familiar enough to be recognized and easily found at the news-stand. This may limit the range of possibilities, yet within that range you can always come up with something new – maybe in the photography, the illustrations, the typography. Usually what does the trick is an intelligent interplay between words and picture. If we're to believe the media analysts, the average attention span at the news-stand is two to three seconds, and so the message must be clear and immediate. Of course this also depends on how the magazine is presented – whether in piles or displayed on the shelf – where it's essential that the message is visible. If the whole cover is displayed, this isn't a problem, but you have to allow for a worst case scenario, and so many magazines have now taken to repeating their logo in small print at the top of the spine.

Harper's Bazaar, No. 2965, 1958, USA

Harper's Bazaar, August 1940, Great Britain

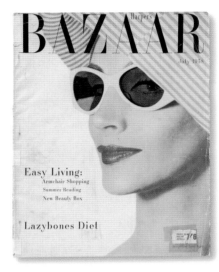

Harper's Bazaar, July 1958, USA

Vogue, March 1945, USA

Vogue, January 1950, USA

Vogue, February 1953, USA

Harper's Bazaar, October 2000, USA

Vogue, November 2001, France

Madame, June 2001, Germany

COPIES AND QUOTES

From pure plagiarism to intelligent allusion

Good ideas are a wonderful thing, and everybody loves them. But what happens when problems arise and no one can come up with an original solution? For many, the simplest way out seems to be battening on to others. Regardless of whether a licence fee has or has not been paid, the rehash always leaves an unpleasant taste in the mouth. Many of these cases are only known to those on the inside, but even if the general public has no idea what's going on, the copy-cat with a conscience will still feel guilty at having failed to find his own solution. The spectrum runs from quoting, through adapting, to outright pinching. All the same you have to admit that, apart from the question of ethics, there's a lot to be learned from comparing similar covers. Even when exactly the same picture is used, there are always differences brought about by the particular design, with logos and text automatically affecting the impact of the picture. The two Jack Nicholson covers for *Männer-Vogue* and *GQ* are a good illustration of the point. In the first one the close-up is hemmed in by the typography, in the other the face is left with room to breathe. The extent to which the pictures themselves have become the subject matter can be seen from the cover of *TV Spielfilm*, in which three models fill the whole page. A few years earlier the same company had used the same photo for the cover of *Max*, but the new version omitted Naomi Campbell. The missing parts of Tatjana Patitz's body were supplied by Photoshop.

Photos were already being tampered with seventy years ago. You only have to think of how they were touched up during the Communist era and also under the Nazis. In those days the process was done by hand and was still pretty clumsy, but today even experts can no longer detect the best work. This, of course, has repercussions on the perception of the truthfulness of the medium, which is increasingly losing the one vital quality it seeks to achieve – its credibility. There is another negative aspect to these modern developments: the widespread use of agency photographs and of CD-ROMs that are free from copyright has resulted in a flattening of their impact. If the same photos appear in ads and brochures and on magazine covers, they'll all inevitably lose a proportion of their individuality.

A feeling of 'take it or leave it' rather than 'look how special we are' is produced. The exchange of ideas can go in different directions, with the editorial side influencing the advertising and vice versa, while the vast reservoir of picture material can serve everyone, from record and CD covers to billboards.

THE CASE OF CAPITAL

Capital was the second biggest publication, after *Twen*, to be developed by the giant of the German magazine world, Adolf Theobald. This new business magazine first appeared in 1961, and like the American *Fortune* its overall concept could be summed up as describing business in human terms, and humans in business terms. The first issues were in a larger format than today, with a black cover and a clear, uncluttered design by Karl Gerstner. In keeping with the content, for decades the cover showed a prominent figure from the business world. In the 1990s *Capital* went international, and it's interesting that in France and Italy, where so many cultural features are held in common, the same subject matter was given a totally different visual treatment. The French edition dispensed entirely with a cover figure and worked only with typographical designs in a popular, almost tabloid style, a bit like posters for a supermarket. The cover of the early Italian *Capital* is the exact opposite: extremely dignified, with a black and white picture of a gentleman in a dark suit. The choice of an elegant, classical font underlines the elitist touch. This noble concept obviously failed to last the course, and in time the vulgarity of the Italian cover came to exceed even that of the French. In order to appeal to the masses, it now parades naked women on the premise that sex sells. Fortunately, the long-serving editor and publisher of the German *Capital*, Johannes Gross, one of the most intelligent people ever to grace the German press, was not there to suffer this humiliation. A Turkish edition is now published under licence, and while the German *Capital* has undergone profound changes in recent years, the Turkish cover continues to follow precisely the same design of coloured areas that marked the German version at the time when the licence was first granted.

Schließlich Wut und Verzweiflung.

Helpline booklet

Focus, No. 44, 1997, Germany

Börse Online, No. 11, 1999, Germany

GQ, January 1996, USA

Männer Vogue, March 1996, Germany

Max Special, No. 1, 1991, Germany

TV Spielfilm, No. 9, 1998, Germany

Der Spiegel, No. 23, 1992, Germany

Focus, No. 19, 1993, Germany

Advertising campaign for milk
(from 1996), USA

Men's Health, June 1996, Germany

Bob Dylan, 'Blowin in the Mind' 1966, Luxembourg (Great Britain)

Adrenalin, No. 9, 2001, Great Britain

Sex Pistols, 'Never Mind the Bollocks, Here's the Sex Pistols' 1977, Great Britain

Brand eins, No. 7, 2000, Germany

Right: Comparing the covers of international editions of *Capital*. Following the precepts of its founder, Adolf Theobald, the cover always showed figures from various sections of the business world. The international licensed editions are sometimes totally different from one another. The biggest contrast is between the French and Italian versions: top right is the supermarket, tabloid-style design of the French, and second row left the elegant, dignified Italian. This dignity seems to have lost out, and since 2001 the Italian *Capital* has followed the principle that sex sells (second row, centre). The Turkish cover design (bottom row right) has preserved the German design that was in existence when the licence was first granted (bottom row, centre).

Capital, April 1976, Germany

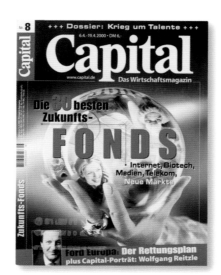

Capital, No. 8, 2000, Germany

Capital, February 1996, France

Capital, April 1997, Italy

Capital, April 2001, Italy

Capital, January 2000, Italy

Capital, No. 12, 1999, Japan

Capital, October 1993, Germany

Capital, June 2000, Turkey

In the 21st century, traditional publishing is no longer the wellspring of innovation

COVERS

The world of magazine publishing has fundamentally changed since the year 2000. It is now theoretically possible to publish almost any kind of magazine, and this new status quo has allowed a lively publishing landscape to grow up across the world. The 'end of print' is now yesterday's news. In Luxembourg, publishers, editors and designers from independent magazines come together every two years for an international symposium, where the creativity of this new generation of magazines is shown to exceed the innovations of traditional publishers many times over.

This new freedom has allowed a thriving and varied range of magazines to develop. Their designs no longer need to follow the traditional rules of the medium. Any form of presentation is possible, and even when archive picture material is used, the results are incredibly striking. Perhaps in years to come, people will speak of the years between 2000 and 2020 as a boom time for the magazine trade.

The stylistic features that mark an era are easier to perceive after time has passed than they are for contemporaries to see, but one fundamental difference between the new independent magazines and their traditional rivals lies in their coding of messages. Easily deciphered motifs on covers are now becoming rarer. Catching the eye is no longer a priority. Many titles want to be accessible above all and avoid empty signals.

One of the pioneers of this new generation of publishers is Oliver Gehrs, who edits the German magazine *Dummy*. Every issue focuses on a different topic and has a different art director.

Oliver Gehrs says: 'The great thing about *Dummy* is having the privilege of being able to print whatever you want, of being able to find stories that can be presented in less-than-obvious ways or that might be considered politically incorrect. It also means building up a network of writers, artists, designers and photographers who enjoy working on something that's a little different from any other magazine.

We get a huge number of pitches from art directors because there's never been a project like ours in Germany before. Normally an art director works for years at the same magazine, so others never get a chance. The style and concept of our magazine gives them a platform that they might have spent years waiting for.

The feedback we've had from readers over the years has almost always been positive. People who get to know the magazine really like it. They love the fact that *Dummy* is more open and more socially relevant, and that it tackles specialized subjects rather than just adding to the pile of lifestyle and mass-market junk. The reception from colleagues has generally been positive too. We know this because they write in and send their ideas. It's really great to be so popular with our peers and to feel trusted by them.

Our job is not only to look at the market, but also to do stuff that we think is politically important. We need to have a stance. Magazines that don't have a moral compass or any political viewpoint aren't interesting to me, personally. The exciting thing is to create a political magazine that doesn't look like one.

I believe that magazines still have a great future, but they need to preserve their authenticity. Magazines really need to come from the heart. They have to get people excited about social issues, and express their meaning clearly. They also need to offer substantial text and great images. Just like vinyl had a resurgence after the CD, quality magazines are also making a comeback.'

There are even a few 'independent' magazines that have found success on the news-stands and within the advertising industry. A supreme example of this type of magazine is *Brandeins* by Gabriele Fischer. From its original status as a niche publication with cult appeal, it has grown to become the bestselling business magazine in Germany. Another notable publication is *Ramp*, which has shown traditional car magazines some very unconventional ways of presenting their subject.

Finally, let's turn our attention to *Cut – Leute machen Kleider* ('People Make Clothes'). This German craft magazine broke all the rules that were seen as vital to the launch of a successful magazine. Even without the power of marketing and advertising, the first print run sold out very quickly, and the reprint soon followed suit. The magazine was lauded in the media and won a plethora of design awards.

This encouraging example shows how, with the help of the internet (*Cut* received a lot of publicity via blogs), the rulebook can also be changed in the analogue world, giving original newcomers to this oversaturated market a real chance at success.

Tokion, March 2009, USA

Soon, April 2007, France

I love you, Fall 2010, Germany

Love, 2009, Issue One,
Great Britain

Sang Bleu, Spring 2010,
Switzerland

Tranoï, 2010, France

Eye, Autumn 2009,
Great Britain

Sleek, Autumn 2010,
Germany

Indie, Winter 2009, Austria

Kultur & Gespenster, Winter 2008,
Germany

Nico, 2010, Luxembourg

Der Freund, 2004, Germany

SVA, 2010, Norway

Mint, 2009, Netherlands

Snob, 2010, Russia

i-D, 2010, Great Britain

WAD (We'ar different), Winter 2008, France

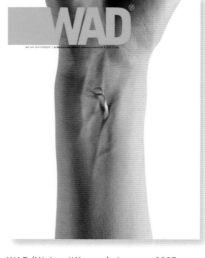

WAD (We'ar different), Autumn 2005, France

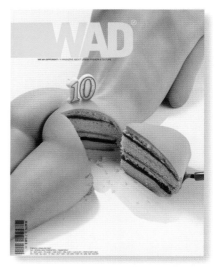

WAD (We'ar different), Spring 2009, France

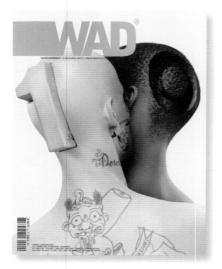

WAD (We'ar different), Spring 2009, France

WAD (We'ar different), Summer 2009, France

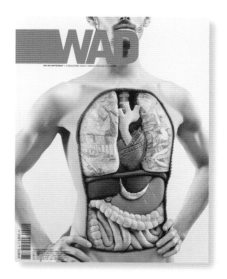

WAD (We'ar different), Spring 2010, France

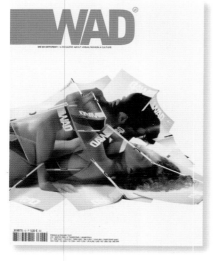

WAD (We'ar different), Winter 2009, France

WAD (We'ar different), Autumn 2010, France

WAD (We'ar different), Fall 2004, France

Dummy, Spring 2007, Germany

Dummy, Summer 2007, Germany

Dummy, Autumn 2007, Germany

Dummy, Spring 2006, Germany

Dummy, Summer 2008, Germany

Dummy, Spring 2004, Germany

Dummy, Autumn 2006, Germany

Dummy, Winter 2006, Germany

Dummy, Summer 2006, Germany

Noi.se, 2003, Australia

Quart, 2010, Austria

Pin-up, Fall 2010, USA

Noi.se, 2005, Australia

Fleisch, January 2009, Austria

Meatpaper, Winter 2008, USA

Meatpaper, Fall 2007, USA

How to, 2007, Germany

Quality, May 2010, Germany

Foam, Fall 2010, Netherlands

Damn, October 2008, Belgium

Damn, August 2010, Belgium

A Magazine, March 2008, Belgium

032c, Winter 2003, Germany

Kinki, February 2009, Switzerland

New Graphic, 2006, China

Dorade, 2010, France

Tickl, 03/2008, Germany

Lurve, Spring 2010, France

Stockholm, 2010, Sweden

Escehaeriefte (Schrift), 2009, Germany

Conditions, 04/2010, Norway

Agora, 06/2010, Germany

Varoom, 09/2009, Great Britain

Objects, 2009, Germany

Mule, 2004, USA

Elephant, Spring 2010, Netherlands

Flaunt, 2005, USA

Snob, 2009, Russia

De:bug, 12/2010, Germany

Arch+, 10/2010, Germany

Fantom, Winter 2010, Italy

Purple Fashion, Fall 2010,
France

Sleek, Winter 2005,
Germany

Nico, Winter 2008, Luxembourg

Drome, 2008, Italy

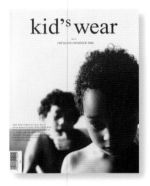

Kid's wear, Spring 2006,
Germany

Rojo, 2008, Spain

Vu Mag, 11/2010, France

Ramp, Spring 2009,
Germany

Tar, Spring 2009, USA

Ambit, 2000, Great Britain

Colors, Autumn 2010, Italy

Tar, Fall 2008, USA

City Magazine, 3/2010,
Luxembourg

City Magazine, 12/2009,
Luxembourg

City Magazine, 5/2010,
Luxembourg

City Magazine, 4/2010,
Luxembourg

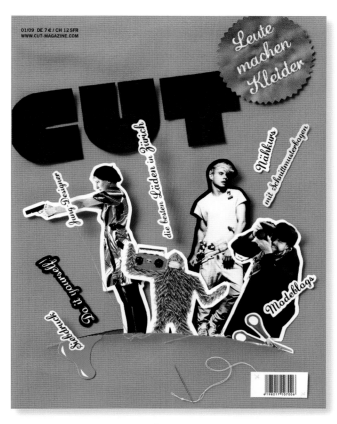

Cut – Leute machen Kleider, 1/2009, Germany

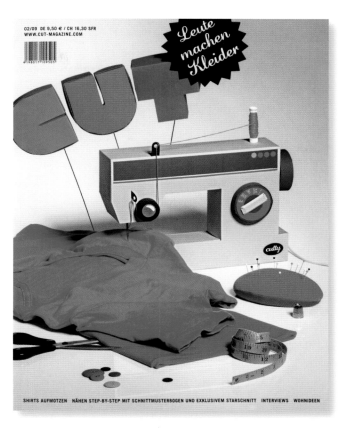

Cut – Leute machen Kleider, 2/2009, Germany

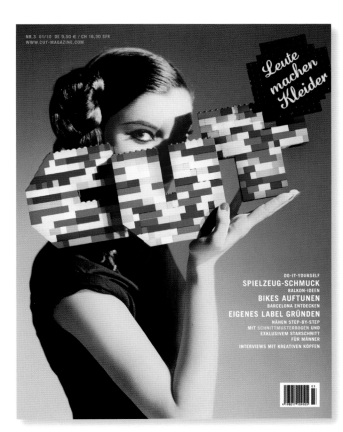

Cut – Leute machen Kleider, 1/2010, Germany

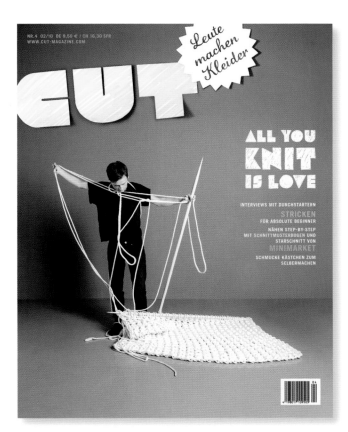

Cut – Leute machen Kleider, 2/2010, Germany

JURASSIC PARK

A film that became a global media event

The film *Jurassic Park* was first released in 1993 and was a worldwide phenomenon that dominated all the headlines. The subject itself was not new, but never before had extinct creatures, in this case, dinosaurs, been brought back to life so realistically.

As always, editors sat down with their editorial boards to discuss the theme of the next edition. For film and video magazines it was blindingly obvious that the cover would mark the opening of the film, but amazingly the rest – quite independently of one another – followed suit: news, science, illustrated, nature, esoteric and satirical magazines all went dinosaur crazy. As picture material was limited, a lot of editors commissioned expensive artwork, but curiously these were not the scientific journals, who mostly made do with stills, but the popular magazines like *Stern* and *Max*. Some tried to grab the reader with cheap horror effects, while others were content to display textbook-style illustrations. Only one magazine rose to the challenge of what in fact was a very complex theme: the cover of *Focus* showed a computer-generated dinosaur climbing out of a screen and mutating into a real creature.

Cinema, September 1993, Germany

Studio Hors Serie, 1993, France

Videoplay, September 1993, Germany

Premiere, November 1993, France

Geo, September 1993, Germany

Dinosaurier, 1993, German special edition, USA

Discover, September 1993, USA

Earth, September 1993, USA

Focus, August 1993, Germany

Stern, September 1993,
Germany

Paris Match, October 1993,
France

Panorama, September 1993,
Italy

Max, September 1993,
Germany

Le Figaro, September 1993,
France

Epoca, September 1993, Italy

Libération, October/November
1993, France

Prisma News, November/
December 1993, Germany

Journalist, November 1999,
Germany

BZ Das Magazin, August 1993,
Germany

Bild+Funk Spezial, 1993,
Germany

Cambio 16, September 1993,
Spain

2000 Magazin für Neues
Bewusstsein, October/
November 1993, Germany

Jurassic Park Comic, No. 2,
1993, Germany

Titanic, September 1993,
Germany

RUNNING JOKES

COVERS

Variations on a self-imposed theme

Readers can sense what motivates a magazine. They
know if it has serious political, cultural or social aims,
and they know if it's been thrust onto the market to
make a quick buck out of a momentary sensation.
Journalists have even been known to go to prison for
their principles.

But it's the subject matter that dictates how interests
are communicated to the reader. The rules that govern
political magazines, for instance, are quite different from
those applicable to the entertainment variety, in which
you often find the technique of the running joke. We all
know this from Alfred Hitchcock, who always made a
very brief appearance at the beginning of his films to
ensure his audience concentrated right from the start so
as not to miss his little cameo. The classic equivalent in
the field of magazines is *Playboy*. The world-famous
bunny turns up on every cover in all sorts of variations
and disguises. Sometimes he hits you in the eye, and
sometimes he's very hard to find, but he's always there,
challenging the reader to solve the visual puzzle. Once
you've let yourself in for this device, you've got to be
certain you can keep it going, and that requires a great
deal of ingenuity. The problem is evident with *Playboy*.
After a highly creative early phase, in which no expense
was spared in the construction of, say, bunny-shaped
chairs or guitars, there have been times when the
powers that be have tightened the corporate belt and
banished the little fellow to buttons and earrings.
Another example is *i-D*. Through all the changing times,
it's a remarkable feat to have maintained the running
joke of the winking eye – whether in photos or comic
illustrations – right through to the present day. The
magazine *George* couldn't keep it up. The idea was to
make a reference to George Washington on every cover,
and this certainly spawned some original ideas, but
evidently inspiration soon flagged and the joke stopped
running. The gag need not be visual. *Loaded* has applied
it to the subtitle. The standard version goes: 'For men
who should know better', and each new cover story
creates a variation on this theme.

Playboy, April 1980, Germany

Playboy, August 1968, USA

Playboy, February 1967, USA

Playboy, March 1980, Germany

Playboy, October 1971, USA

Playboy, July 1980, Germany

Playboy, November 1970, Germany

Playboy, April 1973, Germany

Playboy, January 1982, USA

Playboy, February 1968, USA

Playboy, October 1965, USA

Playboy, September 1974, Germany

I-D, September 1985, Great Britain

I-D, December 1988, Great Britain

I-D, May 1990, Great Britain

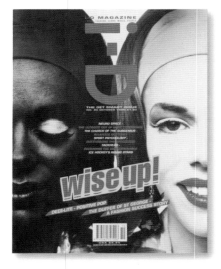

I-D, October 1990, Great Britain

I-D, January 1993, Great Britain

I-D, No. 309, 2010, Great Britain

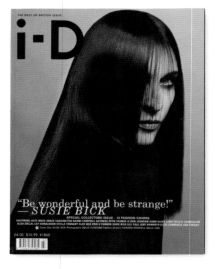

I-D, No. 297, 2009, Great Britain

I-D, February 1996, Great Britain

I-D, July 1996, Great Britain

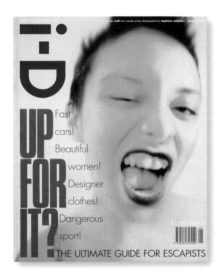

I-D, January 1997, Great Britain

I-D, September 1997, Great Britain

I-D, December 1997, Great Britain

I-D, May 1998, Great Britain

I-D, April 1998, Great Britain

I-D, June 1998, Great Britain

I-D, September 1998, Great Britain

I-D, June/July 2002, Great Britain

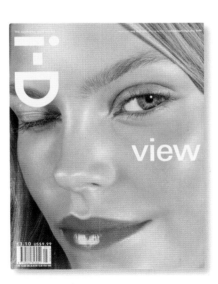

I-D, May 2000, Great Britain

Loaded, June 2000, Great Britain
'for men who should know britters'

Loaded, January 2000, Great Britain
'for girls hugh should know better'

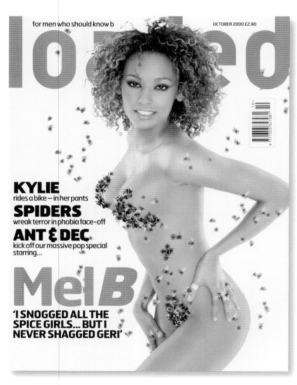

Loaded, October 2000, Great Britain
'for men who should know b'

Loaded, June 2001, Great Britain
'for men who should have butlers'

George, October/November 1995, USA

George, April 1997, USA

George, December 1995/January 1996, USA

George, June 1997, USA

George, June/July 1996, USA

George, February/March 1996, USA

COVER PHOTOS.Portraits

Cover design with the evocative power of the human face

In order to catch the eye, most magazine covers use pictures – generally photos, but occasionally also drawings. The covers reflect the huge range of styles and subjects, and the focal point of interest is humanity, whether in the form of portraits and full-length figures, or in relation to various environments such as architecture or nature. The evocative power of the face is certainly at its strongest when eye contact is made with the reader, and so the magazine strategists naturally make full use of this device. Nearly all women's and fashion magazines design their covers along these lines, and so do those that specialize in erotica. The face is often almost life-size, but there are extreme cases in which the camera has zoomed in to fill the whole page just with the eyes and lips. Another way of attracting attention is to focus on unusual details, or on sophisticated composition. Colour and black and white photographs are used in equal measure. Coloured portraits, so long as they're straightforward, are best suited to popular, more fashionable magazines, while those that are more culturally orientated lean towards black and white. When the subject is someone well known in public life, the choice of picture depends on the type of story to be told. If it's about their unusual life, for instance, the familiar mass-produced press agency photograph won't be suitable, because here the emphasis should be on the unfamiliar, hidden side of the person concerned.

This does not apply to fashion or lifestyle magazines. They use professional models who can change their identity, with the help of subtle make-up and styling, to achieve any desired effect and fit in with any theme.

These faces can convey all nuances and moods, ranging from the romantic to the inaccessible, from an infectious 'joie de vivre' to irradiating eroticism – all of which are evident, for instance, in the collection of Claudia Schiffer covers.

In the sphere of political or financial magazines, there's far less flexibility in the portraits of politicians and high-profile businessmen. Only in exceptional cases will these busy people grant the time for a photo session, and so even the best-known magazines have to make do with stock material. Some opt for a montage or collage in order to convey their message. But even when an exclusive session is granted, the interests of the VIP often clash with those of the photographer or art director. The subject may wish to hide behind the mask of responsibility, while the photographer may seek openness. In any case there's often not enough time for the photographer to form any sort of relationship with their subject. It's entirely the opposite with personalities from show business. Film stars and pop stars live and thrive on the media, and are happy to use photo sessions as a means of establishing their image.

So far only single photographs have been mentioned, but there's also the multi-picture principle. This form of serial presentation is best suited to subjects that deal with a variety of different aspects. The division into small sections may detract from the immediate impact of the cover, but in terms of form it can lead to quite intriguing effects. Typographically, though, such covers pose tricky problems, and the cover lines need to be reduced to a bare minimum.

Vanidad, March 2002, Spain

Noi.se, No. 26, 2011, Australia

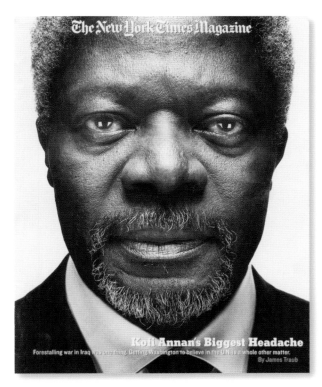

The New York Times Magazine, No. 3, 1998, USA

The New York Times Magazine, No. 8, 1991, USA

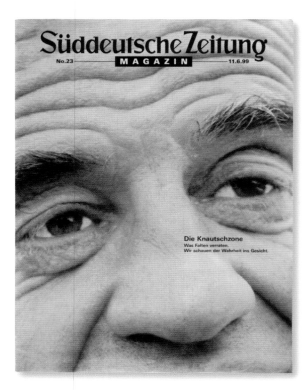

Süddeutsche Zeitung Magazin, June 1999, Germany

Skim.com, No. 2, 2000, Switzerland

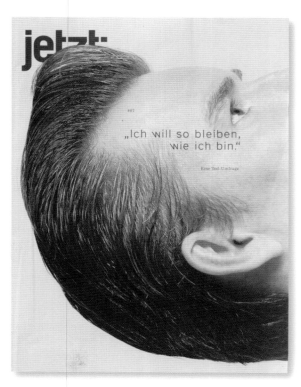

Jetzt, No. 7, 2001, Germany

Vorn, Issue 4, 2007, Germany

Allegra, January 1996, Germany

Domus, October 1998, Italy

Arena, November 1999,
Great Britain

Max, June 1997, France

Tempo, March 1986, Germany

Jetzt, No. 35, 1998, Germany

Die Zeit Magazin, October 1998,
Germany

Süddeutsche Zeitung Magazin,
November 1994, Germany

Donna, March 2002, Italy

Colors, No. 13, 1995 – 1996, Italy

Style, October 2001, Great Britain

Jetzt, No. 42, 2001, Germany

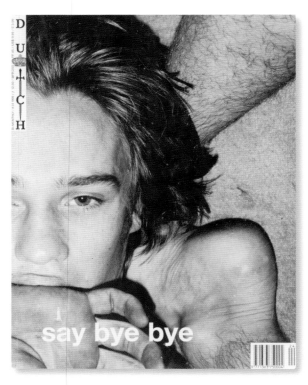

Dutch, No. 24, 1999, Netherlands

Lux, August 1994, Germany

Jetzt, No. 22, 2000, Germany

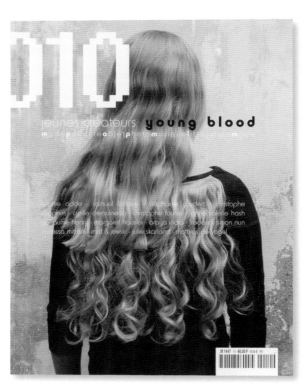

Jeunes Créateurs, No. 127, 2001, France

Quest, No. 21, 2009, Germany

Medical Solutions, No. 01, 2008, Germany

A Magazine, No. 10, 2010, Netherlands

Forum, No. 01, 2009, Germany

Kid's wear, No. 31, 2010, Germany

Deutsch, No. 43, 2010, Germany

TAR, No. 39, 2010, Italy

Colors, No. 72, 2007, Italy

Independent News, 2010, Germany

QVEST, No. 43, 2010, Germany

Vincent, No. 14, 2010, France

Independent News, 2010, Germany

Eyemazing, Issue 1, 2007, Netherlands

Geniş Açi, No. 13, 2000, Turkey

Form, No. 182, 2001, Germany

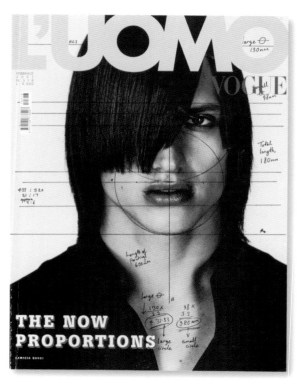

L´uomo Vogue, February 2001, Italy

Kid's wear, No. 17, 2003/2004, Germany

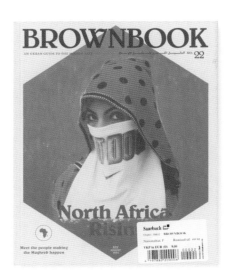

Brownbook, No. 22, 2010,
United Arab Emirates

El País Semanal, No. 1.769, 2010, Spain

Eyemazing, No. 04, 2004, Netherlands

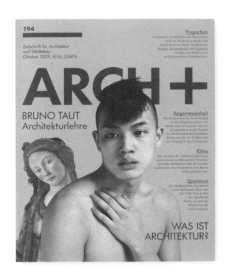

Arch Plus , No. 194, 2009, Germany

Acne Paper, No. 11, 2010, Great Britain

Leicaworld, No. 02, 2006, Germany

H magazine, No. 95, Spain

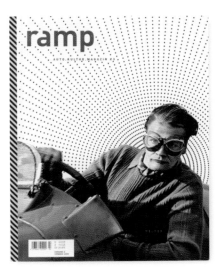

Ramp, No. 03, 2008, Germany

Photo, No. 292, 1992, France

Stern, No. 15, 1990, Germany

Lei, No. 138, 1989, Italy

Tempo, October 1989, Germany

Vanity Fair, December 1994,
Great Britain

Moda, December 1991, Italy

Wallpaper, May 2001, Great Britain

GQ, September 2000, Italy

Madame Figaro, No. 681, 1997, France

Spiegel Spezial, No. 4, 1999, Germany

Stern, No. 39, 1998, Germany

SZ Magazin, No. 41, 2009, Germany

The range of expressions covered by one model,
Claudia Schiffer.

Tomorrow, No. 26, 2000, Germany

TV Spielfilm, No. 25, 2001, Germany

Gala Life & Style, August 2000, Germany

Max, August 1991, Italy

Amica, September 1999, Germany

Zeit Magazin, No. 42, 2010, Germany

Zeit Magazin, No. 42, 2010, Germany

Marie Claire, November 2001, France

Harper's Bazaar, March 1995, USA

Arena, October 1999, Great Britain

W, June 1989, USA

W, October 1995, USA

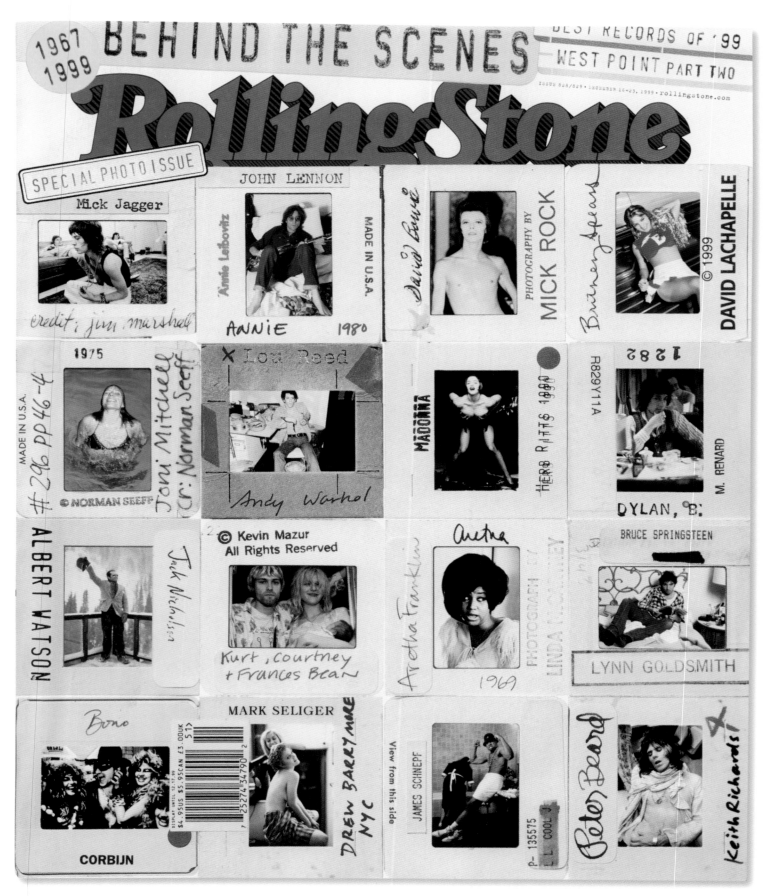

Rolling Stone, December 1999, USA

P, No. 17, 1999, Germany/Great Britain

Brett, No. 14, 2001, Germany

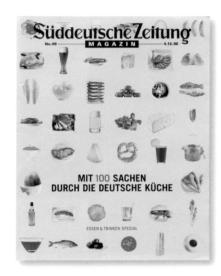

Süddeutsche Zeitung Magazin, No. 49, 1998, Germany

O, The Oprah Magazine, May 2002, USA

FAZ Magazin, October 1998, Germany

Jetzt, No. 8, 2000, Germany

Max, March 1995, Germany

Die Zeit Magazin, No. 35, 1998, Germany

Print, January/February 1995, USA

Zeit Magazin, No. 8, 1981, Germany

Martha Stewart Living, March 2002, USA

Juice, May 2002, Germany

Life, No. 56, 1995, USA

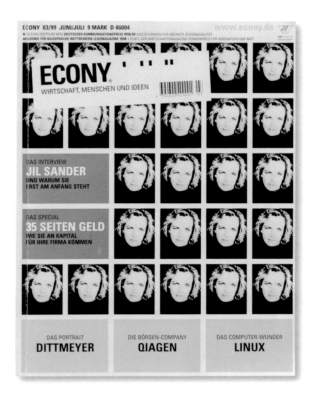

Econy, No. 3, 1999, Germany

Wiener, No. 334, 2009, Austria

Der Spiegel, No. 13, 2001, Germany

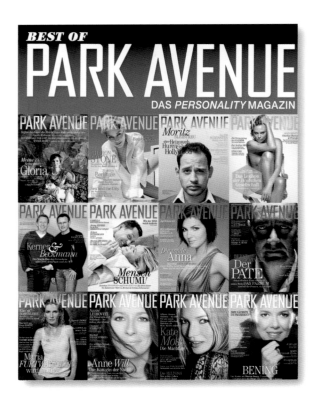

Best of Park Avenue, Special Issue, 2007, Germany

Love, No. 03, 2009, Great Britain

Love, No. 03, 2009, Great Britain

Love, No. 03, 2009, Great Britain

Love, No. 03, 2009, Great Britain

Love, No. 03, 2009, Great Britain

Love, No. 03, 2009, Great Britain

Love, No. 03, 2009, Great Britain

Love, No. 03, 2009, Great Britain

Domus, June 2000, Italy

Domus, February 1995, Italy

Domus, No. 942, 2010, Italy

Domus, No. 940, 2010, Italy

Domus, No. 943, 2010, Italy

Domus, No. 938, 2010, Italy

Domus, No. 939, 2010, Italy

Domus, No. 936, 2010, Italy

Eye, No. 77, 2010, Great Britain

Kaleidoscope, No. 09, 2010,
Italy

BabyBabyBaby, No. 06, 2006,
South America

TAR, No. 04, 2010, Italy

DUF, No. 02, 2010,
Netherlands

Brand Eins, No. 02, 2010,
Germany

Elephant, No. 01, 2009, Great Britain

Leap, No. 05, 2010, China

Foam, No. 25, Netherlands

SZ Magazin, No. 10, 2010,
Germany

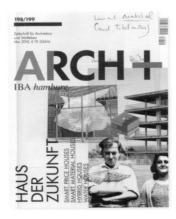

Arch Plus, No. 198/199, 2010,
Germany

Frame, No. 76, 2010, Netherlands

TYPOGRAPHICAL COVERS

The wide range of typographical designs

Magazine covers don't necessarily have to be pictorial. It's also possible to create interesting designs just by using typography. The impact may not be quite so popular, but a wide range of styles are available. Certain filigree forms can have a very intellectual effect, and big, colourful lettering can arouse strong emotions. Computer magazines have become more and more inclined to use nothing but text on their covers, though there's little sign here of typographical sophistication. In this field, the covers are becoming almost indistinguishable, and the only competitive element is the number of subjects they each try to cram in. Character and individuality are nowhere to be seen. One happy exception is the Dutch business magazine *Quote*, which over the years has shown that typography and colour alone can be used to create an attractive cover. Simply by varying the size of the letters, cleverly juxtaposing the lines, and changing the colours, an astonishingly rich range has been created.

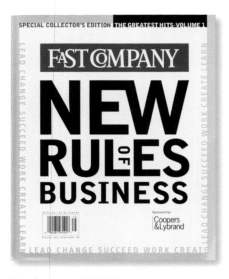

Emigre, No. 54, 2000, USA

Ampers & ND, No. 2, 2001, Great Britain

Artur, No. 16, 1998, Germany

Fast Company, 1997, USA

Vogue 3W, No. 615, 2001, Italy

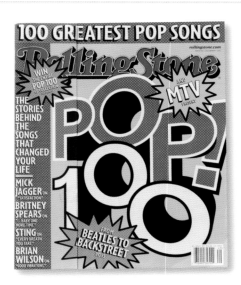

Rolling Stone, No. 855, 2000, USA

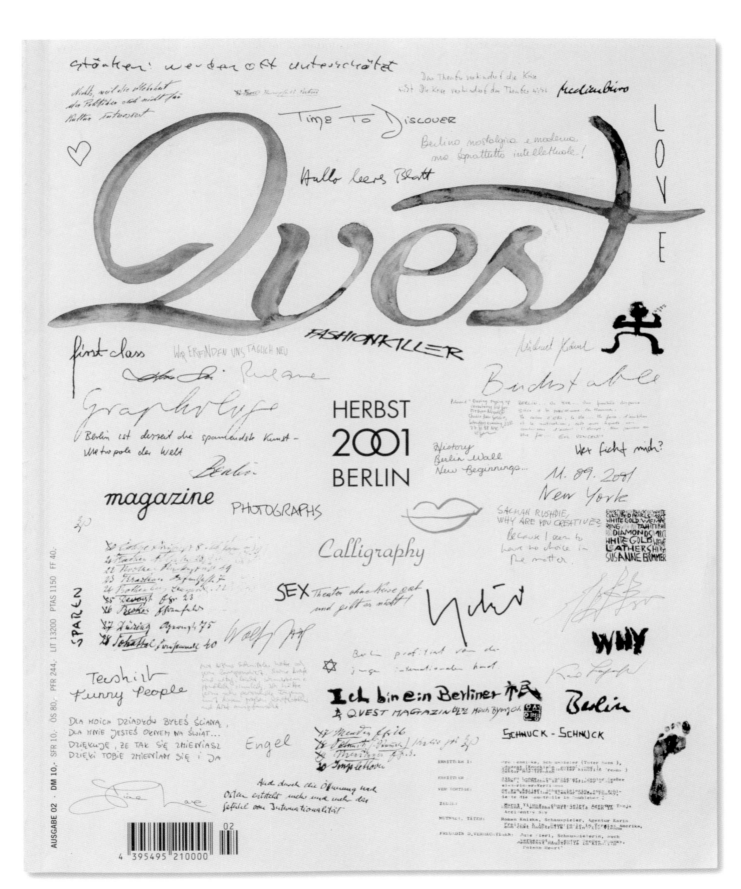

Quest, No. 2, 2001, Germany

Print, May/June 2000, USA

Wired, October 2001, USA

Novum, 02/2006, Germany

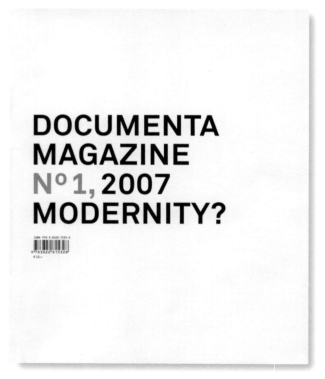

Documenta Magazine, No. 1, 2007, Germany

Wallpaper, February 2007, Great Britain

Material, No. 5, 2001, Switzerland

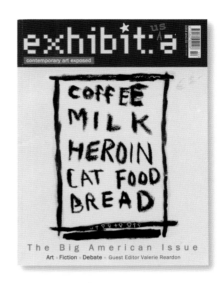

Exhibit:a, June/July 2001, Great Britain

28832 Berlin, October 1999, Germany

Der Spiegel, No. 7, 2001, Germany

Brand Eins, No. 10, 2010, Germany

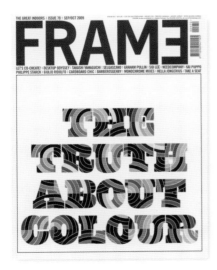

Frame, No. 70, 2009, Netherlands

Greenpeace Magazin, No. 01, 2011, Germany

Items, May/June 2002, Netherlands

Quote, April 1998, Netherlands

Quote, November 2000, Netherlands

Quote, December 1999, Netherlands

Quote, October 1999, Netherlands

Quote, April 2000, Netherlands

Quote, November 1999, Netherlands

Quote, March 2000, Netherlands

Quote, August 1999, Netherlands

Quote, May 1999, Netherlands

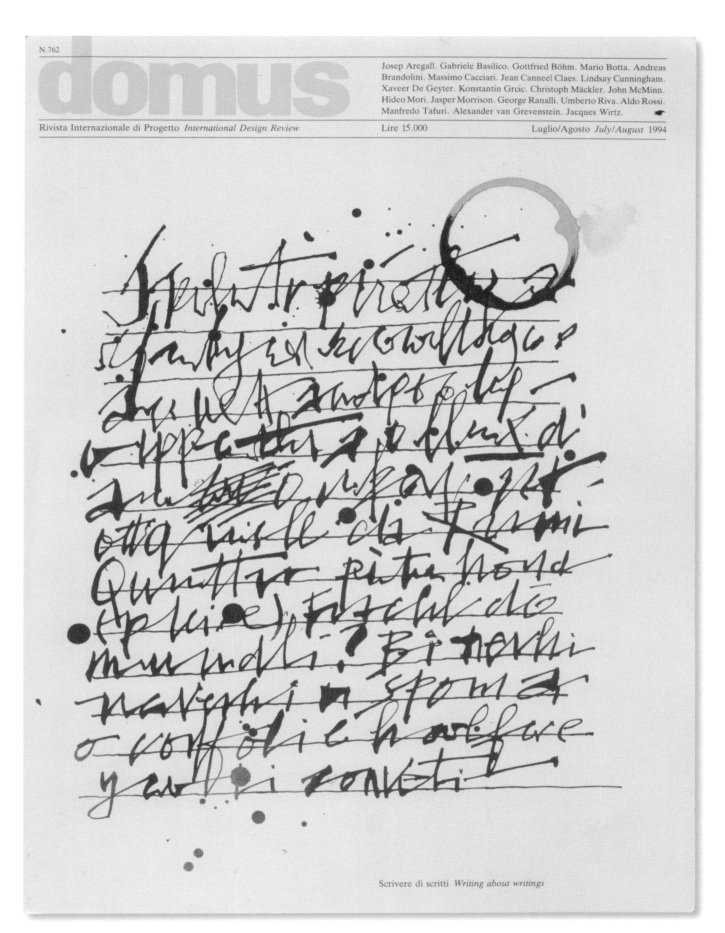

N.762

domus

Josep Aregall. Gabriele Basilico. Gottfried Böhm. Mario Botta. Andreas Brandolini. Massimo Cacciari. Jean Canneel Claes. Lindsay Cunningham. Xaveer De Geyter. Konstantin Grcic. Christoph Mäckler. John McMinn. Hideo Mori. Jasper Morrison. George Ranalli. Umberto Riva. Aldo Rossi. Manfredo Tafuri. Alexander van Grevenstein. Jacques Wirtz.

Rivista Internazionale di Progetto *International Design Review*   Lire 15.000   Luglio/Agosto *July/August* 1994

Scrivere di scritti *Writing about writings*

Domus, July/August 1994, Italy

ILLUSTRATED COVERS

From the realistic drawing to the artistic illustration

The flood of pictures and the levelling effect of photography have meant that anyone who wants to stand out from the crowd has to look for different means of expression. Illustrations are the perfect way to counter the conventional. They're always suffused with an artistic, personal element, and are particularly suited to matters of individual interpretation. An illustrated cover automatically adds a touch of class, and its succinctness of expression makes it more memorable. But the aesthetic elitism of a good illustration doesn't

endear itself to the masses, and so this form remains exceptional. In the 1950s and 1960s there were some extremely popular illustrated magazines with very realistic drawings – the *Saturday Evening Post* in USA and *Hörzu* in Germany, for instance – but nowadays photography is deemed to be more effective. Illustrations are also made use of in political magazines, but they're exceptional and are only there to make comments on particular issues.

Big, No. 23, 1999, USA

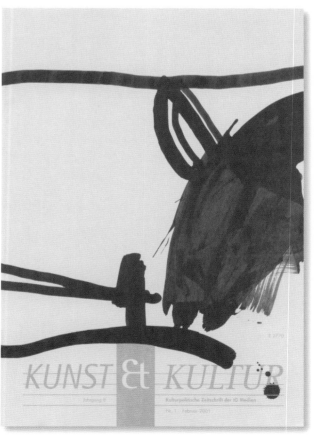

Kunst & Kultur, February 2001, Germany

Der Spiegel, No. 33, 1999, Germany

Brett, No. 10, 2001, Germany

Brand eins, March 2000, Germany

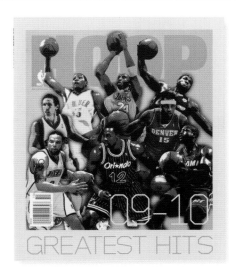

Hoop, No. 06, 2010, USA

Bomb, No. 98, Winter 2007, USA

Be Street, No. 11, 2010, France

SZ Magazin, No. 09, 2010, Germany

Wooden Toy, No. 07, 2010, Australia

Wired, June 1997, USA

HUGE, No. 011, 2004, Japan

Eye, No. 42, 2001, Great Britain

HUGE, No. 041, 2008, Japan

SZ Magazin, No. 53, 2009, Germany

Ad!dict, No. 11, 2001, Belgium

Monday Morning Says, No. 04, 2008, Great Britain

Dada, No. 25, 2000, Netherlands

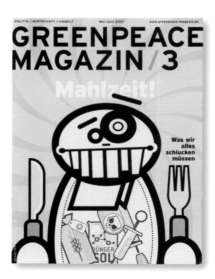

Greenpeace Magazin, No. 3, 2001, Germany

The Believer, No. 03, 2010, USA

Galerie Papers, Issue 12, Spring 2006, Great Britain

The Face, January 2000, Great Britain

SPECIAL FORMS

Magazines with different covers

If you're a creative designer and want to experiment with a magazine cover, you're better doing it with one of the leisure variety rather than with an earnest issue on current affairs. Innovative magazines are nowadays indulging in more and more experiments. The most popular is the creation of a link between front and back covers – for instance, the front showing the front of the model, and the back showing the back. Another interesting variation is to get the same edition displayed at the news-stand with different covers, either quite independent of each other or complementing each other like a kind of puzzle. The object can be to test readers' reactions, or simply to get them to buy more than one copy. *Domus* had a chameleon cover in several different colours to imitate the animal's ability to camouflage itself. One edition of *Rolling Stone* printed five different covers to feature the five members of the band NSync. This method of displaying different covers on the shelf can even be used as a democratic means of influencing public opinion. Liz Jones, editor of the British *Marie Claire*, was concerned about the health risks entailed in the current trend of employing very thin models. For one edition she used two different covers, one with a fuller figure, and one with the usual waif. Apparently it was the fuller figure that sold more copies, but this seems to have had no lasting effect on the modern concept of beauty.

Marie Claire, June 2000, Great Britain (Pamela Anderson)

Marie Claire, June 2000, Great Britain (Sophie Dahl)

Rolling Stone, August 2001, USA

Rolling Stone, August 2001, USA

Rolling Stone, August 2001, USA

Rolling Stone, August 2001, USA

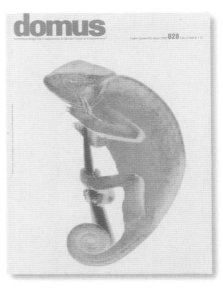

Domus, July/August 2000, Italy

Domus, July/August 2000, Italy

Domus, July/August 2000, Italy

Harper's Bazaar, February 2002, USA

Harper's Bazaar, February 2002, USA

Rails, December 2001/January 2002, Netherlands

Rails, May 2001, Netherlands

Rails, August/September 2001, Netherlands

Rails, November 1997, Netherlands

Rails, July/August 2000, Netherlands

Rails, June 2001, Netherlands

Nanyou/Nüyou, February 2002, Singapore

Spruce, No. 1, 2001, Great Britain

Colors 41, December 2000/January 2001, Italy

Dutch, January/February 2002, Netherlands

Esquire, March 2002, Great Britain

Surface, No. 14, 1998, USA

Magazines are brands just like other consumer goods

An essential feature of magazines is regularity of publication – whether at weekly, fortnightly, monthly, bimonthly, quarterly or half-yearly intervals. What matters to the reader is that the magazine is recognizable, and the prime responsibility for this falls to the trademark, or logo. A classic example is the red masthead with white lettering which, ever since it was started in 1936, made *Life* magazine instantly identifiable all over the world. This form of logo is still the most common to be seen at the news-stand. The original idea was to send out a clear, strong signal, but of course when everyone's sending out similar signals, the effect is drastically reduced. With the great flood of magazines now on the market, logos have undergone a large number of mutations. The masthead, which stands out from the rest of the cover, is now to be seen in all shapes and colours. Its normal position is in the top left-hand corner, because that's the section guaranteed to be visible at the news-stand, no matter how densely the magazines are displayed. Even so, there are variations: at the bottom, in the middle, or even vertical along the left or right-hand sides. The letters are often combined with a symbol, an obvious example being that of the German magazine *Stern*, meaning 'Star', whose masthead consists of a red panel with a stylized white star to complement the title.

Although the rules of the advertising game say that, for psychological reasons, trademarks should never be changed, there are some magazines that make a virtue out of ignoring the rules. A well-known example is *Raygun*, which, during the design reign of David Carson, appeared with a different logo for every issue. The design of the cover was always so different that its very unconventionality became the hallmark of its identity. The mutations of the logos were an integral part of this creative rule-breaking, and in such cases the desire to be original and innovative can justify the slaughter of commercially sacred cows. Of course the rules are not an end in themselves, but are only there as an aid to building and preserving an identity. If this can be achieved by other methods, then no one will complain at the widening of the repertoire.

The masthead, which needs to be clear and concise, usually stands on a different coloured surface to the rest of the text. But even here there are exceptions. If there's no masthead, it's particularly important to choose lettering that will distinguish the logo from the cover lines, which announce the subject matter inside and must be easy to read. A logo is not read, but simply recognized, and since logo and cover lines perform quite different functions, it makes sense to separate them typographically. Many magazines nowadays are quite happy to use existing fonts for logos, although in the past there were periods when they were specially made to measure. There was a rule that one letter in the logo had to be 'wrong', or odd, so that it would be noticed and imprinted on the memory. Anything unobtrusive, uniform, or easily overlooked generally disappears at once from our recollection. Logos that are handwritten or drawn are sure to be individualistic. Of course, they fulfil none of the requirements of objectivity or timelessness, but instead they offer personality and emotion. It's always difficult to find the right balance between the modern and the classical, but generally the more modern or fashionable the logo, the shorter its life will be, while the more classical or neutral it is, the less striking and expressive it will be. The classical solution is always stigmatized with a sort of wishy-washiness, and can never endow its magazine with any sort of individual character. One significant criterion for the effectiveness of a logo is the link between form and content, and this can be vividly illustrated by the following example of two logos that follow the same principle – that of *Blond* and that of the German film magazine *Schnitt*, which means 'Cut'. The letters of both logos are cut off at the bottom. In the first case, the device simply plays with form and has nothing to do with the content; in the second, a typographical equivalent is created for the cutting of the roll of film which gives the magazine its title. The parallel here between logo and subject matter is therefore far more striking.

Blond, March 2002, Germany

Schnitt, March 2000, Germany

Internet World, March 1996, USA

Focus, May 1997, Germany

The device of sliced letters applied to logo design: in *Blond* it's purely decorative, while in *Schnitt* it directly complements the title.

Using nothing but conventional fonts for a logo can cause problems. Ideally, the logo should be so unique that it cannot be used in a different context by another magazine.

Arena, Jan./Feb. 1988, Great Britain

Arena, December 1997, Great Britain

Arena, December 2001, Great Britain

Arena, June 2002, Great Britain

The mutating logo of *Arena*: originally it sprang from a font designed for *The Face* and later transformed into 'Typeface six' by Neville Brody. In time, only the characteristic A remained from the original.

When computer magazines are named after a particular system, their existence is naturally bound up with that system. An interesting case is the magazine *DOS*. Once the system had become obsolete, the name had to undergo a process of modernisation. The change took place in stages, with 'DOS' getting ever smaller, until *PC Magazin* took over entirely.

DOS, No. 8, 1996, Germany

DOS, No. 10, 1996, Germany

PC Magazin DOS, No. 12, 1996, Germany

PC Magazin DOS,
No. 1, 1997, Germany

PC Magazin DOS,
No. 3, 1997, Germany

PC Magazin DOS,
No. 5, 1997, Germany

PC Magazin DOS,
No. 2, 1998, Germany

PC Magazin,
No. 7, 1998, Germany

Life, April 1954, USA

Sowjetunion, No. 7, 1979, Russia

Star Revue, October 1957, Germany

Paris Match, No. 500, 1958, France

Bunte Illustrierte/Münchner
Illustrierte, No. 50, 1960, Germany

Triunfo, June 1963, Spain

Hayat, May 1966, Turkey

Wienerin, Autumn 1985, Austria

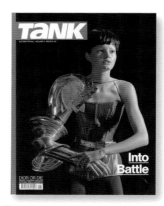

Tank, Vol. 4, Issue 8, Great Britain

The Face, June 1990, Great Britain

Spy, March 1992, USA

Man, January/February 1997,
Netherlands

Baby, April 2001, Netherlands

Achtung, No. 8, 2007, Germany

1585, No. 1, 2006, Germany

AM7, No. 7, 2001, Germany

Wallpaper, January 2007, Great Britain

Aria, No. 5, 2006, Italy

Pool, No. 17, Austria

Edit, No. 27, 2002, Germany

Placed, January 2007, Austria

Fluter, No. 21, December 2006,
Germany

Interni, No. 3, March 2007, Italy

Feel Good, No. 3, 2002, Germany

Raygun, March 1994, USA

Raygun, February 1994, USA

Raygun, November 1994, USA

Raygun, April 1993, USA

Raygun, September 1996, USA

Raygun, September 1993, USA

Raygun, June/July 1994, USA

Raygun, May 1994, USA

Raygun, November 1993, USA

Raygun, October 1995, USA

Raygun, October 1993, USA

Raygun, April 1995, USA

Raygun, March 1993, USA

Raygun, March 1993, USA

Raygun, September 1995, USA

Raygun, October 1994, USA

Raygun, February 1993, USA

Raygun, June/July 1993, USA

Big, No. 33, 2000, USA

Big, No. 26, 1999, USA

Details, February 1989, USA

Details, November 1989, USA

Details, December/January 1990, USA

Big, No. 35, 2001, USA

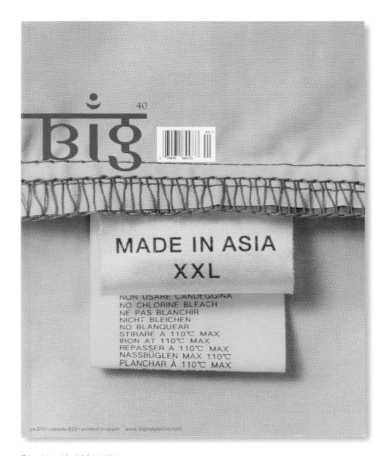

Big, No. 40, 2001, USA

Details, February 1990, USA

Details, June 1998, USA

Details, March 2002, USA

Interview, January 1990, USA
(see index for credits)

Madison, January/February 2000, USA

Backspin, March 2002, Germany

Flaunt, No. 5, 2000, USA

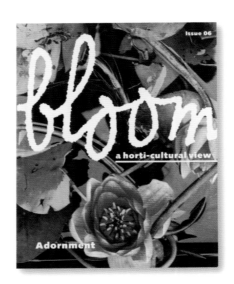

Bloom, June 2001, France
Cover photo by Sarah Allen

M-real, Winter 2001, Great Britain

Wohnrevue, No. 3, 2006, Switzerland (Logo by Matteo Thun)

Wohnrevue, No. 4, 2006, Switzerland (Logo by Antonio Citterio)

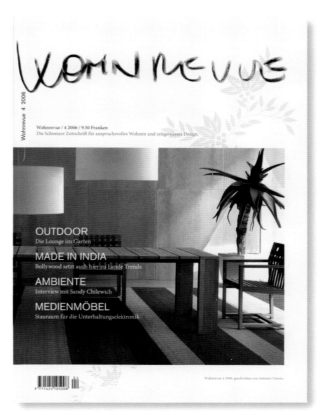

Wohnrevue, No. 5, 2006, Switzerland (Logo by Piero Lissoni)

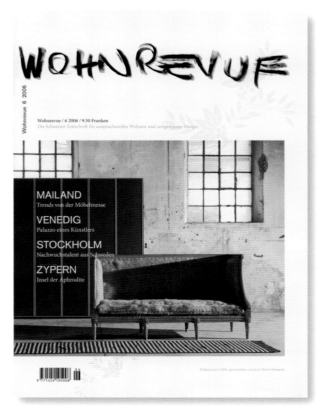

Wohnrevue, No. 6, 2006, Switzerland (Logo by Jean-Marie Massaud)

Blvd., April 2000, Netherlands

Polaroid, No. 13, 1997, Germany

Super Lodown, No. 30, 2002, Germany

Massiv, No. 6, 2000, Switzerland

Street, January/February 2001, Austria

High Potential, April/May 2001, Germany

Nest, October 2000, USA

Speak, Winter 1998, USA

h4, January – March 2000, Singapore

Seventh Sky, November 1999, Switzerland

Passport, September 2000, Switzerland

Trans-form, 2001, Great Britain

Constructional aspects of a magazine feature

In designing the layout of a magazine feature that's to cover several pages, you first have to decide what visual elements (photographs, illustrations, charts, and so on) are to be used to accompany the text. Naturally, the selection must fit in with the content, and here the ideal example is a report illustrated with photos by a single photographer. It's more difficult when the pictures stem from different sources, and in this case you need to choose photos that have plenty of stylistic features in common. The more heterogeneous the pictures, the less harmonious the layout will be. Is it possible to combine coloured photographs with black and white? They might complement each other, but only if they can still be related to elements of the text – for instance, with a recipe, in which the preparations are shown in black and white, and the finished dish in colour. If there's no logic behind the choice, the effect will be messy. With articles on politics or business, the mixture of photos and charts is often unavoidable. An article might begin with a large-scale portrait – photo or drawing – and then continue with various charts, which would then create a good balance. Magazines on current affairs generally have to use a wide variety of picture material, but the priority here lies with the information and not with purely aesthetic considerations.

As soon as you know how the feature is going to be constructed and what pictures are available, you can design the opening section. With longer articles, it makes sense to begin with a double page to set the right tone. This spread should touch on as many aspects as possible so the reader can decide whether or not they want to read the rest. If you want to open with a large picture, you'll obviously go for the best one you've got, but it must be representative of the whole article and not just one tiny aspect that will be irrelevant later on. To what extent it should be a teaser depends on the designer, but again it's important to strike a balance between arousing the reader's curiosity and not giving the whole game away at the same time. Mike Meiré often begins with rear views in order to get his reader to turn the pages until they finally see the face.

The vital typographical element at the beginning of any article or story is the combination of headline and standfirst. This form has found favour all over the world. Ideally, the headline should be exciting, but it must tie in with the opening without merely duplicating what's about to be said. The standfirst, which forms a link between headline and text, will be more informative, but again it must arouse curiosity without telling the whole story. The headline/standfirst format is both binding and liberating, and can also be supplemented by other forms of heading. Where justified, the author and photographer can be given due prominence after or even in the standfirst. Whether the actual text should begin on the opening page or not depends on the overall composition, but it's certainly better to launch the reader into the feature straight away, rather than having a break in continuity before they turn the page.

Econy, No. 2, 1999, Germany

Econy, No. 1, 1998, Germany

HOW NOT TO GET STARTED

A few dos and don'ts

1. OFF THE PEG

After the winner of an open competition has turned down the job because the conditions are totally unacceptable, a young pair of graphic designers, 'SunnyMoonMouse', are commissioned to design a visual concept for a brand new in-store magazine. They have to come up with the following: one editorial page, one double-page list of contents (but single-page if they like), a double-page of reports, and a longer feature that opens with a double-page spread and continues for two more pages. The proprietor wants to have a three- and four-column format, three types of chart (one pie, one bar and one graph), and of course two cover designs with variations, including a logo and sample pages complete with stylistic models. The typefaces must be delivered along with all of these. The designers can go ahead and copy the banderole idea proposed by the sixth-placed competitor because, in the words of the marketing director: 'You can't copyright things like that.' A total of eight working days will be allotted, and all rights will be the proprietor's. With the first issue, the design team should just 'have a look', as a sort of service-cum-favour, but from No. 2 onwards, the magazine will be put together in-house. The company has had twelve picture CDs copied by its own advertising agency, and if necessary it can always hire a digital camera. The 48-page magazine will be compiled by two girls from the marketing department for whom the company has splashed out on a desktop publishing course.

You can make magazines that way. No problem. But why bother to bring in designers at all, since nowadays there's a huge selection of dirt-cheap model layouts and graphics available by the cartload?

2. MADE TO MEASURE

Don't hold a competition. A competition is just another way of saying that there's nobody in the company who knows the market well enough to make a decision. Instead, this is what you do: a competent member of staff has a close look at all the top names in the world of corporate publishing. In order to remain anonymous, they order one magazine or another through the firm's advertising agency, study the yearbooks and ads contained in Forum Corporate Publishing's factbook, and make notes while studying the imprints of the magazines chosen. After much humming, hawing, profound thought and mature reflection, they then make the decision. Alone and unaided. An appointment is made for a getting-to-know-you session. The more cautious-minded will opt for a team that's already been active in the field, or has even specialized in this particular section of it, while the more enterprising will take on someone who's totally new to it. In this way you can hope for fresh ideas and new approaches, although of course it's essential that the designer should have had adequate experience. Let someone else pay for the learning process and its sometimes nasty consequences. After all, nobody is infallible. Provided you get on, and agreement can be reached on the size of the salary, work can begin. Generally, there's already an overall concept defining the aims of the company and the new magazine. The next step is for the designers to become familiar with the character, philosophy and ambiance of the company that's taken them on. Their perception will never again be as objective as it is during this first phase, because later they'll become just as entangled in the business as everyone else, and so it's important that the first impression should also be a lasting one. Once the aims are clear, you can make some tentative initial designs – tentative because you can never expect to get it right first time. As with the perfect made-to-measure suit, there always has to be tiny adjustments here and corrections there. When the first few pages are ready, it's time to consider the technical details: what format, what paper, what texture, and maybe refinements, embellishments, distinguishing features. As soon as matters of colour and typeface come under discussion, corporate design must also play a role, and an inexperienced newcomer will give the game away by insisting on designing the magazine quite independently of what's already to hand. Of course, magazine design follows very different rules from those governing business reports, shop-fittings, prospectuses, the sides of trucks and the stands at trade fairs. That's only right and proper. The whole point of magazines is that they should give a more objective slant to information, and there shouldn't be even a whiff of self-promotion. Despite this, though, the overall impression created by the company's various public outlets should not be diffuse. Very few companies ever make their mark with just one single message, but the clearer and simpler the messages, the more distinct the impression will be, while too great a diversity will blur the image. It's vital for colour, pictures and text to be integrated in a single unifying concept. Even if the rules that govern business prospectuses and so on cannot be applied to magazines, which go by a more flexible, variable code, it's still essential for the magazine to be recognizable. The balance between recognizable sameness and attractive difference is an extremely fine one. One major problem is maintaining consistency in a company's colours. As there are far more firms than colours that can reasonably be registered as trademarks, you have to make sure that the chosen shade is always reproduced with absolute precision. Many financial institutions, for example, favour blue, and so the particular shade must be the same on everything that appears in public – whether in print, on the screen, on signs, on visiting cards, or at trade fairs. A further complication here is that of reproducing special colours through four-colour printing. This is a daunting prospect, as will be confirmed by anyone who has seen the Pantone range of four-colour comparative values, but for this problem too there are new solutions. There have been many recent developments with pigments, adhesives, and the software for scanners and printing-presses. The Aniva process, for instance, which is especially suitable for company publications, has greatly improved the accuracy of four-colour printing in reproducing special colours.

Anyone who's not happy with standard solutions to these problems – knowing full well that sooner or later things are bound to go radically wrong – but who sets out to find new and better ways, will certainly need time. The same applies to the choice of typeface. Generally, when a typeface is selected for corporate design, people don't think of magazine design. Countless tests are necessary in the quest for the right type, regardless of

such details as the way the company's name is to be written in the text as opposed to the logo. Harmonization of fonts can only be achieved by practical experimentation, for such problems can never be solved theoretically. As far as pictorial language is concerned, it's extremely difficult to find anything new, and your old stock material is certainly not going to do the trick. We grasp pictures in a different way from the way we do texts, and they can very rarely convey the message intended by the company. When the pictures are of people, even the man in the street, hardened as he is by the ubiquitousness of posters, ads and TV commercials, can distinguish what is staged or posed from what is genuine.

Since there are virtually no monopolies, no company can afford to ignore competition. It often happens that rival firms will quite unscrupulously take over a good design or an original idea. Perhaps once in a blue moon a designing equivalent of Mozart may burst upon the scene, effortlessly creating the most complex and harmonious themes. But they're the exceptions that prove the rule. It generally requires vast amounts of time and effort to produce anything even approaching the perfect composition. Balance and coordination, and concealment of the time and effort involved, in practice mean a process of endless reshuffling, streamlining, adjusting and adapting. The design comes to life through variety and contrast – round alternating with square, hard with soft, rough with smooth, big with small, colour with black and white, elaborate with simple. Without wishing to labour the musical analogy, you could say that only someone who can conduct the full orchestra of typography, colour, line and surface, photography and illustration will be able to give full dynamism to the complex score that constitutes a magazine.

Magazines are individuals that can mature into strong personalities, and in whose presence you feel at home. The more original and surprising they are, the more time you want to spend with them. Featureless display dummies, waxwork dolls, faceless non-entities that radiate blandness and dullness – these can never create the bonds of friendship. A dull magazine is a paper scarecrow that can serve only to drive its readers away.

The dual strategy of free and compulsory content, and its typographical variations

Although there's a huge range of headline/standfirst combinations that any article can be opened with, in practice virtually every variation has the same underlying pattern and structure. In its classic form, the headline is the freestyle exercise, open to the creativity of its author. It should stimulate associations in the reader and arouse their curiosity. Sometimes it may allude to well-known titles of books, films or songs, though all too often this can seem clumsy and laboured. A trio of examples which successfully play on the double meanings of words springs to mind:

1) 'Der Brandenburger Tor'. The brainchild of Ferdinand Simoneit, former editor of *Spiegel*, this headline refers to Axel Caesar Springer's *Bildzeitung,* which raged against the student movement of the late 1960s. The apparent reference to the famous gate in Berlin is deceiving:'das Tor' means 'gate', but 'der Tor' means 'fool'.

2) 'Ohne Waters alles Roger'. When Pink Floyd parted company with their creative genius Roger Waters, everyone thought they would fold – but they didn't. The headline reads 'Without Waters Everything's Roger' – that is, OK.

3) 'Waiting for Bordeaux'. This article on the length of time it takes for a good red wine to mature employed the image of a stage set with spotlights shining on empty glasses – reinforcing the allusion to Samuel Beckett's play *Waiting for Godot.*

Such headlines don't convey any precise information, but they create a certain tension. The counterpart to this freestyle is the compulsory exercise – in this case, the standfirst. Here the subject matter is pinpointed, but without destroying the tension or giving away too much of the content. Now the reader can decide whether to go on or not. In special interest magazines, though, this technique is used far less frequently. The standfirst functions as a summary, and the article that follows springs no surprises but merely goes into detail.

The variety and sophistication of typographical forms that can be applied to this combination of headline and standfirst are astonishing when you remind yourself that they all have the same basic structure. The most common deviation from this basic structure is to combine both parts in a single text, or to make one flow into the other. Evidently there has been little effort to devise any radical alternatives.

1/4 nach 5, No. 5, 2002, Germany

Harper's Bazaar, September 1992, USA

Vogue, February 2000, Italy

City Magazine, July 2000, China (Hong Kong)

Spex, No. 7, 2002, Germany

Adrenalin, No. 7, 2001, Germany

Details, No. 2, 2002, USA

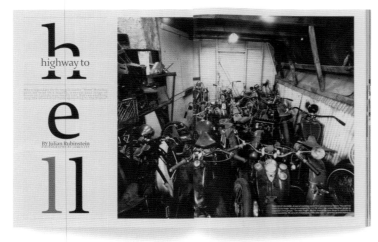

Details, No. 3, 2002, USA

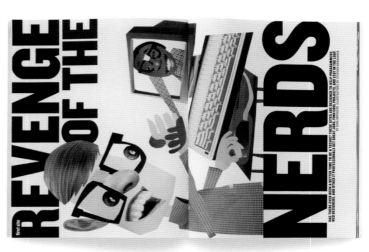

Fast Company, May 2000, USA

Style, December 2000/January 2001, Germany

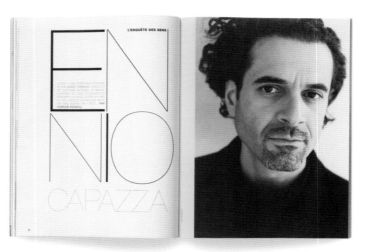

Mode Max, No. 7, 2002, France

Substance, January/February 2001, Singapore

Esquire, Autumn 2001, USA

The Face, No. 7, 2000, Great Britain

TEKST HUB DE SWARTS EN BETTINA VOGE · FOTO'S ABO PRICES · ABP / TRANSWORLD

MARCO PIERRE
WHITE
KING OF FOOD

Hij is de jongste kok in de geschiedenis van Michelin die drie sterren kreeg en de enige
Britse ooit. Recent zei hij te stoppen met koken – zich uitsluitend op het management
van zijn restaurants te zullen richten. Het leverde een waar tumult op in het Verenigd
Koninkrijk. Maar Marco Pierre White is niet het type om er uit te stappen. Hij had vooral ook tijd nodig om te bedenken wat er mondiaal culinair echt staat te gebeuren. ▷▷▷

Man, January/February 2000, Netherlands

Style, March 2002, Germany

Cine Chart, July 2000, Germany

Vogue, August 2000, Italy

Esquire, No. 5, 2001, USA

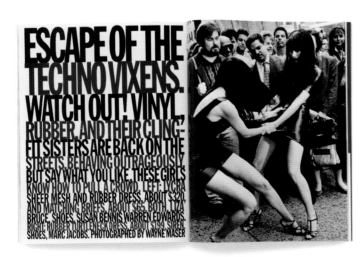

Harper's Bazaar, August 1994, USA

Harper's Bazaar, August 1994, USA

Esquire, No. 2, 2000, USA

Style, April 2002, Germany

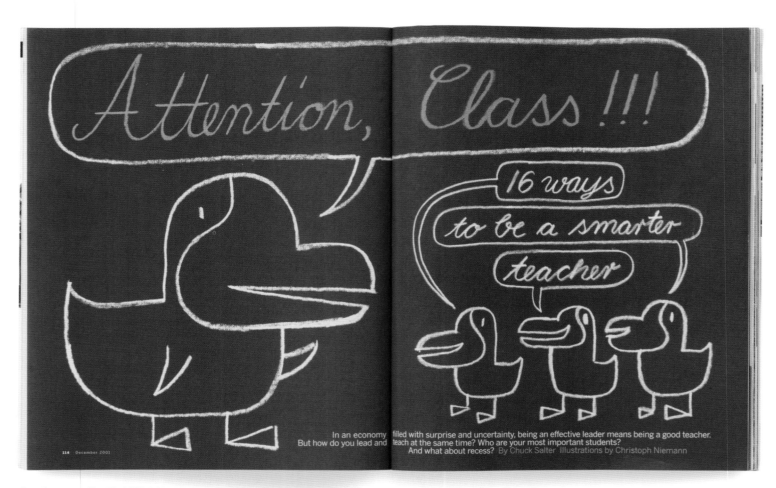

Fast Company, No. 53, 2001, USA

Fast Company, July 2001, USA

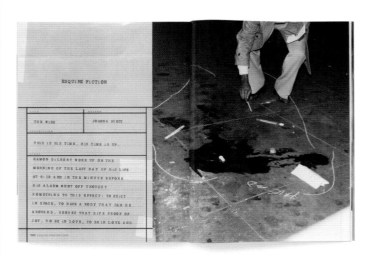

Esquire, No. 2, 2000, USA

Esquire, No. 2, 2000, USA

Fast Company, November 2002, USA

Rolling Stone, April 2000, USA

Speak, Winter 1999, USA

A useful navigational device

As Henri Nannen, founder of *Stern*, once remarked, magazines can be constructed like surprise packages. When they are, you don't need section divisions. The reader doesn't look for anything in particular, but simply allows themself to be surprised by the discovery of something interesting. Such a method would be totally unsuitable for a specialist magazine, and indeed the more informative a magazine sets out to be, the more essential it is to give it a clear and easily accessible structure. Section headings are extremely helpful in guiding the reader around. Normally, the area at the top of the page is the best place for these headings. Whether it's useful to combine them with a special colour code will depend on the size of the magazine; for instance, if there are 36 pages with six sections, different colours would be pointless, since some of the sections would probably only contain one article. One important

decision is whether to use single terms or to give a double reference – you might, for instance, put a whole section under the heading of 'Culture' and supplement this heading with the particular theme dealt with on each page. It doesn't matter a great deal whether the two terms are positioned next to each other, one above the other, or separated by lines; what matters is that the main heading and subheading are easy to recognize. There's a broad repertoire of forms for these headings, including coloured areas, bars and lines, to name but a few, and these are sometimes also used in combination with icons. If there are colours, the question arises whether they should also be taken up in the articles themselves, and if so, in what form. If such patterns are overdone, they can quickly become uninteresting, and so as always, the art lies in finding a discreet balance between consistency and variety.

Ad!dict, Spring 2001, Belgium

Music

KRONOS QUARTE

25 Years (Nonesuc
Arguably the most
ble of our time, Kror
anniversary with th
revitalized the strin
ing and premièring
repertoire includes
composers as well a
man, and Muddy W
sifiable musicians li
Their execution o
its precise metric sh

¡CUBANISMO!
Reencarnación (Rykodisc)
Originally conceived as a one-
shot, all-star recording project,
¡Cubanismo! has evolved into

Wired, February '3000', USA

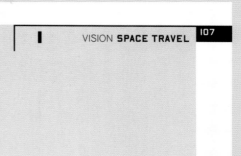

Premium, No. 3, 2001, Germany

Vogue, November 2001, Italy

ur mom
then to
nt. Then
y.

attend?

school,
her, fifth
oyed it.

myself and in my friends, but all of a sudden I'm in
another room. Now, if fourteen people come up to
you and say they have a script—you suddenly turn
into that guy going, "Please give me a break!" You
want to be the guy that says, "Oh, your project is
great. How can we make that happen?" But then
you're getting so much attention, you end up

Details, March 2002, USA

Wired, June 2000, USA

▶ quelqu'un qui résiste, c'est
formateur. Le pouvoir qu'c
les adultes, de les obliger à
pour l'évolution de la socie

DS, October 2001, France

Squeeze, April/May 2001, Netherlands

IQ Style, September 2001, Germany

CODE.34

text_amy andrieux
photography_ben watts

Notting Hill

Trace, No. 34, 2001, USA

objekte | online.universum | multimedia.zo

internet-broking

Mac Magazin, March 2000, Germany

22 **SPECIAL**

Pur, Autumn 2000, Germany

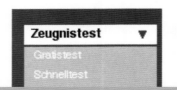

Trainer fürs Assessmen

Zeugnistest ▼
Gratistest
Schnelltest

Wer zu einem Assessment Center (AC) eingeladen wurde, hatte bislang drei Möglichkeiten: 1. unvorbereitet

realistischen Pr
druck, unerwar
tionen zu meis

Junge Karriere (trade paper), March 2002, Germany

chtscreme gegen Augen-
ne angeschwollenen Fes-
bringen sollen. Heute be-
auf: Kosmetika, Kleidung
urch weniger anfällig für
jar eine Flasche Wiesen-
vom Roomservice, gleich
n, damit der Smog von
verden kann. Also zum

3.2
.CONVENIENCE

Text **Susanne Baust**
Design **Rainer Pirker**

Susanne Baust ist
Motorjournalistin und

Copy, November 2001, Austria

20.04.-20.05.
TAURUS THE NATURALIST
Flowers: pink rose, poppy, lavender
Perfume: Green Tea by Elizabeth Arden
Labels: Gucci, Louis Vuitton, Prada

Blouse, £360, by **Tom Ford** for **Gucci**
Jacket, £420, by **Tom Ford** for **Gucci**
Skirt, £280, by **Tom Ford** for **Gucci**
Bracelets, from £60, by **Pebble**
Ring, £140, by **Pebble**
Emerald ring, £1,200, by **Celia Forner** from **La Joya**

Spruce, Spring/Summer 2002, USA

crafts ● WINTER VILLAGE

door panel

Martha Stewart Living, December 2000, USA

pop	rock	punk	metal	dance	hiphop	funk

ontladen, zonder plat te worden. Midden in de dubieuze eighties-revival grijpt Spacer terug op de jaren '70 met immer verrassende breakbeats en virtuoos jazzspel in de Herbie Hancock-traditie. Maar *The Beamer* is geen moment pretentieus of bombastisch. Onmisbaar voor DJ's en een stevige aanrader voor thuisluisteraars die meer willen dan eenduidige dansmuziek. RUTGER VAN WEL

Oor, April 2001, Netherlands

Wired, February '3000', USA

CineChart, November 2001, Germany

Details, March 2002, USA

Mutabor, No. 10, 2002, Germany

Martha Stewart Living, December 2000, USA

Wallpaper, May 2001, Great Britain

Vogue Paris, February 2001, France

Buch Journal, Autumn 2001, Germany

TYPOGRAPHY.Page Numbers

The basis of orientation in magazines

Page numbers are the most basic functional component of any magazine. With their help readers should be able to find their way round the content, but first they need to actually see the numbers – and that's not always easy. The bigger the magazine, the more difficult it is, because generally the thickness is due to a preponderance of unnumbered ads and supplements. Or alternatively, the designer's creative talents have been focused on an element that really should not be the object of their love of experimentation. If you want to spare your reader the pangs of frustration, put your numbers at the bottom of each page, either on the outside or in the middle. In newspaper design it's the top that's favoured, and if your magazine is divided into different sections, the top is also a possibility. In fact nowadays both positions – top and bottom – are equally common. What's really confusing is when both numbers for a double-page spread are put together on just one page. Let's face it, the wheel cannot be reinvented or improved, and similarly any deviation from normal pagination can seem artificial. Even experimental magazines sometimes have to make use of the basics.

IdN, No. 8, 2001, China (Hong Kong)

Mixt(e), No. 9, 2000, France

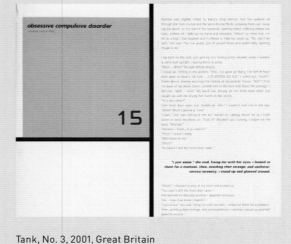

Tank, No. 3, 2001, Great Britain

Pop (The Face), Spring/Summer 2002, Great Britain

002_Zeina al-Hajj

„Wir nehmen es nicht
hin, dass sie giftigen Schlamm
ins Mittelmeer pumpen."

003_Nedim Goletic

Der Koordinator des Kosovo-Hilfe-
programms von Cap Anamur
während einer Einsatzbesprechung

„Ich träume davon,
mit Serben und Albanern ein
Dorf aufzubauen."

Greenpeace Magazin, No. 1, 2000, Germany

BEAUTY SCOUTS
How Bookers Choose a Model Face

Arude, No. 12, 1999, USA

[EASTCHIC]

Multi-tiered white
gold & diamond
choker, worn with
matching bracelet &
ring all by **Bulgari**.
Vintage t-shirt
(Opposite page:)
Multi-strand pearl
necklace with sapphire flower clasp
worn with ruby
flower brooch all by
Asprey & Garrard

72

Surface, No. 32, 2001, USA

h war richtig glücklich.
te. Der Tango hat mît uns gemacht,

15
17
19
21
23
25
27
29
31
33

deren
und ich habe wieder auf

Artur, Summer 1997, Germany

Meticulo
minimalis
response
solution.

Footnote:
*Indeed, i
only in m
from deve
dominate
client pur
for this A

36 iSh

Ish, August 1999, Singapore

genot.
ur is niet altijd
nce nooit per-
telling, waarbij
lbaar is. Dan is
n te vertoeven.
aam. Eigenlijk
et mensen kun-
Bij film moet je
: mee, maar ik
zet mij schrap
? Doe maar. Ik
is naar de set

It. In de kern is
il dat iedereen
op gezelschap.
el vriendelijke
van melancho-
er mij gezegd:
d hij wel mooi.
I kon hij omge-
nog nauwelijks
denis. De knal-
... daar word je

Als acteur had ik meer uit mijn fysieke mogelijkheden moeten
halen. Ascese is het grootste streven. Ik wilde een top-
acrobaat worden, maar die discipline heb ik nooit kunnen
opbrengen. Nu ben ik eigenlijk best tevreden met mijn lijf.
Mijn kop wordt beter. Dat gaat dan vooral om film, om de
camera. Vroeger wenste ik dat mijn gezicht beweeglijker was.
Dat ik meer spiertjes kon commanderen, al was het maar het
optillen van een linkerwenkbrauw. Zo kun je makkelijker een
emotie laten zien. Ik moest dus alles van binnenuit laten
komen, ik moest door een diep, doorwrocht dal gaan om de
emotie eruit te stuwen - en zo tot de juiste expressie te
komen. Nu gaat dat wel. Dat is de genade van het ouder worden: mijn gelaat is veel beter in staat om emoties te verbeel-
den. Een gunstige evolutie.
Voor de rol van de ultieme slechterik Dreverhaven in *Karakter*
zou ik te goeiig zijn. Dat zijn mijn ogen, dacht ik meteen.
Daarin zit de tristesse, de melancholie. Er moest iets kouds in.
Het licht moest eruit. Dat kun je bereiken door op een lichte
manier te loensen, en je blik te fixeren op één punt. Ik heb
dat vaak geoefend voor de spiegel.
Tijdens het draaien was de camera-
man zo getroffen door het effect dat
hij een lampje op de camera zette
om mijn ogen op te lichten. En ik
maar proberen om mijn ogen dood
te krijgen! Het heeft toch goed

45

Rails, November 2001, Netherlands

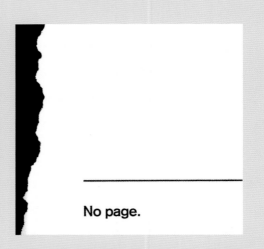

No page.

RE, Spring 2001, Netherlands

band uit twee broers: toetse
zanger Johhny Blake (20). M
meer dan een band. Een hel
designers, fotografen en styl
rondom hen geschaard. Verg
Warhol en zijn Factory zijn o
de kleding schakelden ze Fe

024

Squeeze, April/May 2001, Netherlands

Artur No19
noch 10 Seiten

Artur, Spring 1999, Germany

Style, February 2001, Germany

Jeunes Créateurs, No. 6, 2001, France

Ifans knows he could be called all three. He can't do anything about it. And he doesn't care. The movie industry is, after all, its own kind of circus. You run away and join it, no matter which roles you choose.

The place Ifans has run away from is Wales. He was born and raised there but moved to London when he was eighteen. "I found it

just go
saying "
"I don't
budget's
"But I t:
to the h

This
Hallströ
Shipping
Julianne

Black Book, Spring 2002, USA

Different methods of indicating the start of a text

In formal terms, the initial letter (or letters) naturally signifies the beginning of the text. The art of illuminated lettering reached perfection especially in religious books between 800 and 1450. The first letter would be large and impressive, richly embellished, painted in glowing colours and partly gilded. The direct opposite of this is the Bauhaus technique of the 1920s and 1930s, which radically reduced the importance of the initial letter, not only out of antipathy towards the decorative, but also out of hierarchical considerations. Jan Tschichold, however, who was an enthusiastic missionary for Bauhaus ideas, actually reverted in his old age to classical typography, which included the special first letter.

It's possible to distinguish, for example, between the following forms:
• The initial that covers two to five lines.
• The initial that starts on the first line but juts out high above it.
• The initial that stands outside the column.

In the US a different form has become very popular: printing the first three words in block capitals. The repertoire has also been extended by the use of arrows and other symbols. At the beginning of the twenty-first century, special initials are no longer in vogue, but the chances are that this trend will change again, and giant letters like those of Willy Fleckhaus will eventually make a comeback. Their effectiveness depends not only on size, but also on the choice of script. Should you use the same font as in the rest of the text, or deliberately draw attention to the initial by using a different font? And should you only use this at the beginning of the text or repeat it at the start of every paragraph? These are decisions that must be taken in the context of the overall typographical design. From a technical point of view, you need to bear in mind that QuarkXpress does not allow for a great deal of sophistication when it comes to the layout of initials within columns. It's therefore a good idea to give the initial a text box of its own. The size of the first letter should fit in nicely with the headline and the text itself; if there's not much difference between them, the effect can be ugly, especially if they're very close to one another. It's become common practice now to have headline and initial the same size and in the same font, but this isn't very attractive aesthetically. The combination of different fonts demands a high degree of typographical self-confidence. In an unpublished literary supplement for the Swiss magazine *Weltwoche*, the initial letters were set as individual notes – a bit like the cadenza of a violin concerto – together with an otherwise pure, classical typography. They were the only form in which emotion and interpretation were given expression.

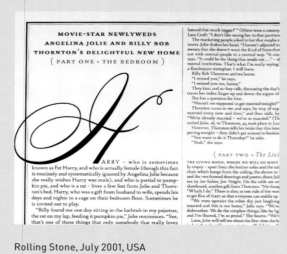

Rolling Stone, July 2001, USA

Detour, Autumn 2001, USA

Für die

Falls Ihr ein wenig mehr Zeit und Mu

Die MTV-Cops Crocket und T
nicht ganz zu Unrecht als d
änderten auch Drehbücher a
Nebenrollen und Glenn-Frey
müssen wir aber auch bald
Goldenen Achtziger zuende,
deutschen Fernsehsender mu
verschiedenen Gründen sehr genau überlegen
oraphisch-soziologischer Natur: Amerikane

Brett, No. 9, 2000, Germany

---

as the

arrival of new, fashion and pop
magazines on the media scene reaches fever pitch, it is time for an eva
This large group of small publications has profoundly affected the
mainstream media and advertising, serving as the latest ground for visu

It started as a curiosity in the 1970s and '80s; the houses and advertisers? Most profoundly, what purpo-se is it all serving? And most critically, can it last? million individuals and total annual c
creation of pop culture magazines by a handful of visionaries prepared to offer an innovative, avant-garde take on fashion in contrast to the oligarchy of the mainstream press. Their view of the world, often inspired by the look of the street and the culture of the night, was a defiant and radical departure from the reigning spectrum of fashion publications in its refusal to stay between the lines of Hollywood gla-mour and catalogue chic. But from a counter-culture manifestation aimed at the few and disenfranchised, the niche press has matured into a full-bodied medium of its own. Its pioneers, titles like, Interview

To be sure, the attention focused on independent magazines recently, has done its part to swell their ranks. Widespread technology has completely revo-lutionized publishing—quite obviously online, but in print as well—to the point that anybody with a com-puter, a contact-laden PR pal, and a dream can start a magazine. A visit to 0fr, the leading Paris-based distributor for style-conscious, cutting-edge publica-tions, reveals mountains of these books; some that regularly and consistently present their evolving nme estimated roughly at $10 million to a single issue of American Vogue.

Regardless: though individually sm that these publications are a major hing the limits of creativity and f Typically built on the intuition of a c tors, art directors, photographers a magazines are strong, highly pers and visions of the world as shared b Their liberation from the pressures (tability to a higher corporate rule ev take risks and often controversial a

Selfservice, No. 14, 2001, France

BROWSER WARS

NOT SO LONG AGO, ON A COMPUTER NOT SO FAR AWAY, YOU COULD
DESIGN FOR THE INTERNET IN THE RELATIVELY SAFE KNOWLEDGE THAT
EVERYTHING WOULD PROBABLY WORK...

The concept of "Internet time" is an odd one. Broadly speaking, it refers to things moving so fast that it's hard to keep a handle on them. While it's most often used to refer to the business side of the Internet and the problems facing companies trying to keep up with technology, it's increasingly just as appropriate for users as well.

In the beginning, the Web was pretty simple. We were all pretty much using the same browser – NCSA's *Mosaic* – and Web pages were simple HTML affairs with a few graphics. Whether you worked on a PC, a Macintosh or a Unix workstation, life looked pretty much the same for everyone. Bandwidth wasn't an issue (although having connectivity at all might be!) and you didn't have to worry about having the right plug-ins when you visited a site.

That was ten years ago now, and even without the idea of "Internet time", that's a long time in technological terms. Many things have changed since then, some for the better, some for the worse. The evolution of NCSA's *Mosaic* into *Netscape Mosaic* and then *Netscape Navigator* was one change for the better. The development of alternatives to NCSA's browser helped spur on the development of the

Cre@te online, April 2001, Great Britain

---

fiction

PSYCHIC

written by **Terese Svoboda** illustration by **Kristian Russell**

The aunt doesn't want to show me the shoe. It's too much like you're a dog, she says.

That's okay, I say. I'd like to take another look at the snapshots.

As the sister flips through the album for the place, the boyfriend says, no, no—wait a minute, here's how she signed herself, and he pulls out a scrap of paper ripped off a letter with Love still stuck to it.

Both the aunt and the sister rear back like the corpse is still curling the *e*.

Flaunt, Spring 2001, USA

→ **NATÜRLICH** zu einer Zeit, als - möchte man den Veterane
ben - in Brasilien noch Milch und Honig flosse
ganz normaler Alltag für den betuchten Mittelstand war, den d
→ mit Marcos teilten. Für Joao Gilberto, Vinicius de Moraes, Ba
Regina und viele andere Bossa-Nova-Künstler, die Ende der f
→ musikalischen Zirkel bildeten, war das Leben nicht schwer. N
Clubs, Bars und Theatern, musizierte gemeinsam und tauscht
Musiker aus wohlhabenden Familien kamen, hatten sie eine
→ genossen, gehörten zur intellektuellen Oberschicht Rio de Jane
mit profanem Geldverdienen zu beschäftigen. Valle: "Der Boss
→ Sommer, Strand und dem Rio-de-Janeiro-Gefühl." So konnte m
ren, in Musikschulen Unterricht nehmen oder geben. Doch t
waren die Bossa Nova-Musiker auch der Musik der Armenvierte
Sambatrommeln auf klassischen Instrumenten nach zu empfinc
ter auch Funkelemente zu erweitern, war zwar nicht klar formu
aber bald als stilübergreifendes Merkmal des Bossa Nova hera
traditionellen Samba verändert, erweiterte ihn um reichere H
und eine andere Rhythmik", weiß Veteran Valle zu berichte
Gesangsbetonung lehnten sich an die perkussive Musik mi
Wurzeln an. Weil es für Derartiges keinen eigenen Namen gab
Beschreibung eines Journalisten, der über dieses "neue Ding"
Marcos Valle betrat die Bossa-Bühne ein wenig später als Jo

Style, June 2001, Germany

François Tru

"he first time I saw *Jules et J*
beginning and I didn't catch th
were two men in love with the same wor
never fought. They spoke about passic
laughed a lot. That night I had to go out,
asking around though and everyone told
Truffaut called *Jules et Jim*. The funn
different ways to describe it. For some, (

Another Magazine, Spring/Summer 2002, Great Britain

SCHLAF!

ES WAR ERST JANUAR, ALS WOLFGA[NG]
AUS DER ERDE KRABBELTE. WELCH [
FRAU KALLERT AUS POTSDAM IHN (
VON *NATALY BLEUEL* FOTO: *GERE*

W[olfgang] kam viel zu früh.
Drei Monate zu früh. Am
Mittag des 29. Januar krab-
belte er in der Nähe von
Potsdam aus der Erde. Genau in dem
Moment, als Gabriele Kallert nach
Hause ging. Sie erkannte, dass unter
dem Erdhäufchen, das sich bewegte, ein

Dingen zuge[
plötzlich so
wärmsten Ta
ren. Die M
cafés, lächel[
Stimmung
flunker. Und
gezuckelt. V

Süddeutsche Zeitung Magazin, March 2002, Germany

Letter from New York / Geoff Nicholson

[H]i Martin.

You want to know what's wrong with America? I'll tell you what's wron[g with]
America. Cheese is what's wrong with America.

Okay, so Switzerland has had five hundred years of brotherly love, dem[ocracy,]
peace and boredom, but at least they managed to come up with one or tw[o]
cheeses. America has had two hundred and some years of revolution, ci[vil war,]
racial conflict and world domination; and all they've managed to come up [with is]
Monterey Jack – a cheese that if it got its act together and improved its fla[vour by]
about two hundred per cent could just about compete with the most m[
soapy English supermarket cheddar.

Every hill and valley in France can come up with its own speciality che[ese

Ambit, No. 161, 2000, Great Britain

Snow, No. 2, 2002, Germany

Every rose has its thorn, and Rosie Perez,
who is back this fall in three new films, has
thorns that are sharper than you might think.

TEXT Alex Wagner   PHOTOGRAPHY Georgia Kokolis

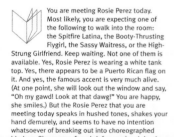

You are meeting Rosie Perez today.
Most likely, you are expecting one of
the following to walk into the room:
the Spitfire Latina, the Booty-Thrusting
Flygirl, the Sassy Waitress, or the High-
Strung Girlfriend. Keep waiting. Not one of them is
available. Yes, Rosie Perez is wearing a white tank
top. Yes, there appears to be a Puerto Rican flag on
it. And yes, the famous accent is very much alive.
(At one point, she will look out the window and say,
"Oh my gawd! Look at that dawg!" You are happy,
she smiles.) But the Rosie Perez that you are
meeting today speaks in hushed tones, shakes your
hand demurely, and seems to have no intention
whatsoever of breaking out into choreographed
hip-hop. She seems, for a brief second, subdued.

Black Book, Autumn 2001, USA

MARC NEWSON

a[

[A]ls er één designer is waarvan we in
de toekomst veel mogen verwach-
ten, dan is het wel deze van oorsprong Australische Engelsman.
Op z'n zesendertigste heeft hij al zo ongeveer alles ontworpen
wat je kunt bedenken: van horloges, afdruiprekjes en flessenope-
ners tot en met meubels, fietsen, auto's en vliegtuigen. Hij
bedient zich van een aanstekelijke en inmiddels invloedrijke stijl,
een actueel soort futurisme, dat naadloos aansluit bij alle jonge
hippe stromingen van dit moment. Marc Newson is ◊peens ont-
dekt als dè nieuwe design-ster van nu, terwijl hij toch al een dik-
ke tien jaar hard bezig is.
Vooral een futuristische auto voor Ford en de private jet waar-
voor hij het interieur en het grafisch design van de buitenkant
verzorgde, bezorgden Newson de nodige sterrenstatus. En hij
heeft ook alles in huis om zich als een echte ster te presenteren.

op z'n
niet ve
volgcu
lag. H
zich a
meube
elkaar
smokk
een na
het va
Toen
veel 'c
lierrui
fabriel
zelfs e

Man, March 2000, Netherlands

THE HEARTBREAKING WORK *of*
AMERICAN LITERATURE

"We were just [
saying to my b[

[D]ave Eggers, a young man already semi-famous as the editor and publisher of the
[maga]zine *Might* in the early nineties, has gotten a six-figure contract (for starters–T[he
Observer reports that he just got $1.5 million for the paperback rights, plus that
movie) and a lot of favorable publicity for his first book, *A Heartbreaking Wor[k of Stagger-]
ing Genius. AHW* (as we will refer to it for the balance of this article) is "bas[ed on a true]
story": the story of how Eggers, the third of four children, lost both parents to c[ancer when he]
twenty and took on the responsibility of raising his youngest brother, then eight y[ears old.

The New York Times loves it. It's been extravagantly praised in two feature articles beside[
favorable review. Michiko Kakutani, the *NYT* fiction editor, said: "At their best, writers
ge[...]combine a mandarin love of ornate, even byzantine prose with the vernac[
of the streets, tossing together the literary and the colloquial with hyperventilat[
they've tackled the crazy, multifarious reality they see around them head-on, try[
all its information-age effluvia willy-nilly into the pages of their books (which)...[
rumors of the novel's demise...are vastly exaggerated."

And yet what's funny about this praise–actually, maybe it's not funny at all–is that examples o[

Speak, Summer 2000, USA

Artur, Summer 1998, Germany

Rolling Stone, June 2000, USA

A way of dividing up long texts

Longer texts can be structured through the use of subheadings, of which there are two basic types. The first is determined by the content of the article and denotes the start of a new segment. From a design point of view, this type of subheading cannot be shifted. The second type is movable, and can be inserted wherever the designer feels it should go. Its function is to create an optical break in the mass of text, and so its content must be less precise because the text will, so to speak, flow round it.

Spex, No. 8, 2002, Germany

Rolling Stone, February 2002, Germany

Brand eins, February 2000, Germany

Mixt(e), No. 9, 2000, France

d

Uno

De Degas contó John Berger que después de decir que hay amor y una vida de trabajo y un solo corazón él eligió y puso su corazón en su vida de trabajo. Boris Pasternak escribió: "Si el lector continúa con esta frase, empezará una tormenta de nieve". William Blake dio antes otro salto mortal: "Quien desea y no actúa engendra la peste", que no sé hasta qué punto cortó la hierba para que Albert Camus hablara del "divorcio entre la mente que desea y el mundo que decepciona". Degas y Blake eligieron, Pasternak convocó su tormenta entre los abedules y Camus se estrelló antes de que hubiera consumado la decepción de su deseo. Hay santos de tu devoción y santos de tu desdén. Las frases hechas son campos minados. Vienen a la lengua impulsadas por halcones tan peregrinos como el de la pereza, el desdén, la necesidad, la desesperación e incluso la melancolía, un agente no consolidado entre los enemigos del capitalismo. Demasiado laxo para ser considerado como un terrorista de confianza, demasiado sutil para que se sacuda el barro de los zapatos cuando los analistas esparcen sobre el damero maldito las condiciones objetivas y las otras. Roald Dahl no es santo de mi devoción, pero dice: "Sólo los hombres jóvenes estallan con violencia, creo que por estar aburridos. Pero en general el ser humano no es muy agradable. No es un animal bueno". Descifrar a Isaac Albéniz no es lo mismo que descifrar a Roald Dahl. Para descifrar a Albéniz no basta con saber tocar el piano. Para descifrar a Dahl basta con tener algún sentido. Cinco dedos no son cinco sentidos. Las frases fuera de contexto son más fáciles de descifrar que los discursos íntegros, igual que no es lo mismo descifrar la *Suite Iberia* que *Rondeña*, ni recordar lo que sabemos mientras escuchamos que comprobar lo que sentimos mientras vemos el mar desde el hotelito azul de la Isleta del Moro, acabamos de casarnos, no hemos dado cuenta de nuestro soberano error y nos aferramos a *El sentido de la vista* para descifrar el tiempo que hace fuera y el tiempo que hace en nuestro interior. También Rafael Sánchez-Ferlosio, este santo de mi devoción, tal vez porque tiene poco de santo y aborrece las devociones, sobre todo las que le suben a él a la peana, aunque sea una peana cívica y de palosanto, o incluso de palo de limonero, blanco luminoso y flexible, dijo una vez que "ojalá" tuviera el dentro un "buen animal". Damos palos de ciego y parece como si diéramos luz a cuartos cerrados. Tragaluces donde el cerebro lleva siglos estibado, envuelto en fardos negros de hule y duelas. Damos de comer a nuestra melancolía y desciframos dos palabras, como si la palabra animal dividiera el mundo en dos, en diez, en doce, en dividendos que dieran trigo como a veces dan los sueños.

Dos

Dice Roald Dahl que el niño ve a los adultos como "unos gigantes. Todos los adultos que rodean a un niño, desde padres a profesores, les dicen continuamente lo que deben hacer. Los niños siempre verán a los adultos como enemigos porque al nacer uno está incivilizado y el proceso para hacernos personas civilizadas es doloroso, difícil y hostil. Si tú tienes que escribir libros que gusten a los niños debes estar de su parte, contra los mayores. Este es el secreto para escribir libros para niños".

(La primera recapitulación de dados y des dice: devoción, desdén y desesperación, tras pasar por la estación del deseo que destila decepción. Y sigue así, pero saliendo del espejo hasta este lado de la nada: debes, difícil, doloroso, dicen y dan dividendos, es decir: doce, diez y dos. El columpio colgaba del nogal no del dondiego ni del dátil, y con el rumor del mundo y del invierno, mientras mi abuela deambulaba entre los espantapájaros de la higuera y del maíz, y cantaba: dividiera, desciframos, damos. Las galletas de coco como una forma de alquilar el hórreo vacío y frío del mundo. Si aquí das un salto mortal puede que dudes y en esa duda te pierdas y te rompas la crisma. Pero sin duda no hay circo y menos teatro. Eso es la escritura o ese es el juego de las divisiones, de uno en uno, de dos en dos, de tres en tres, hasta darte cuenta de que esta no era la dirección que habías pensado tomar cuando pensaste en Dresde, Dios, dinero, don, diezmo, Danubio, dalia, dedicatoria, decimal, durante, día, después, domesticar, Dublín, dulce, diario, dinosaurio, delfín, Duero.

Dos otra vez: por un lado Dallas/Texas, por el otro Guy Debord. Pero veamos cómo se barajan estas cartas que nunca dan dos ni tres ni todo lo contrario, mientras jugamos a vernos en el espejo, es por la mañana, es por la tarde, nos damos una vuelta por nuestras devociones, nos casamos, nos descasamos, nos masturbamos, nos amamos, nos desamamos, partimos el pan como lo hacía Dios vestido de Jesucristo jugando a los dados del destino, partimos en tren como partía Miguel de Unamuno, con una mano en el corazón y la otra en el junquillo de los sueños. Es el turno del discurso de Michel Baier, que dejó escrito: "La moral de *Dallas* representa la justificación de las reglas de intercambio: todo don debe tener un contra don". Su argumento sigue después de un punto y aparte, que en este caso es como uno de aquellos pasos a nivel de Kiev bajo el disfraz del comunismo, bajo la nieve sucia que pisó Walter Benjamin en Moscú mientras dudaba acerca de cómo escribir acerca de Goethe y Asja Lacis le decía que sí y que no al mismo tiempo, y todas las ventanas encendidas en los edificios hablaban de una melancolía proletaria tan temprano, tan temprano. Hace catorce años que Michel Baier dejó escrito en un diario que ya no es el que era (aunque me temo que ninguno fuimos jamás los que creímos ser, los que fuimos aunque lo dijéramos y halláramos fotos que parecen corroborar con nuestro aspecto lo que pensábamos pese a lo que decíamos): "Una moral semejante" (la moral de *Dallas*, conviene recordar después de tanta agua dura y panzuda bajo los puentes) "se adapta perfectamente a la idea que todos tenemos de Texas. Dallas es la ciudad donde se ha cometido el parricidio por excelencia: el asesinato de un presidente. Todos se toman la justicia por su mano, en contra de las leyes más fundamentales. Texas concentra en un sólo lugar el pasado y el presente de Estados Unidos: el pasado, con la conquista del Oeste y los ranchos; el presente, con el mundo de los negocios y el petróleo. Así, viendo el folletín, los estadounidenses vuelven a vivir la formación de su sociedad: todavía no se ha consolidado la moral; tiene que vérselas seriamente con la inmoralidad. Pero una moral semejante también es universal". ¿Qué pinta aquí *Dallas*, con tan poquitas des para paliar la duda de si dorar la píldora con dudosas maniobras para que la página sea duradera?

Ahora que los medios de comunicación de masas se han convertido en agentes de festejos del pensamiento único sacamos a un suicida del armario de su propio olvido y leemos sus palabras como si el mar no borrara una y otra vez la antigua pizarra de arena y Guy Debord no se hubiera arrancado de cuajo de este lado de la pista de patinaje. "El espectáculo es la ideología por excelencia, porque expone y manifiesta en toda su plenitud la esencia de todo sistema ideológico: el empobrecimiento, la sumisión y la negación de la vida real". Qué mejor ejemplo que el de la devoración de África, convertida por los medios en una constelación de volcanes en erupción, que deslumbra primero y abruma después, pero que no explica el contenido de la historia ni el reparto de las culpas, no sólo grabadas en los hombros de los colonizadores, sino también a prorratear entre muchos africanos que se convirtieron en los más entusiastas practicantes de una nueva colonización de sus pueblos. África como líquido de revelado. El dramaturgo de Congo-Brazzaville Sony Labou Tansi fustiga a los africanos a través de su personaje de Mallot en *Je soussigné cardiaque*: "Nos hemos vuelto los mayores productores mundiales de vacío. Nos hemos equivocado de vacío. Nos hemos equivocado de independencia. Brutalmente equivocado". Pero desde nuestro lado en el bastión de fabricantes de realidad vendemos cada vez más entradas para el partido incomprensible del mundo. Como el mundo es oscuro e incomprensible jugamos al futbol y a hacernos ricos para olvidar que hace tiempo nos arrebataron el lugar en la historia. Ya que no queda nada que hacer, dividamos el tiempo entre trabajo y diversión. No volverá Carlos Gurméndez a aguarnos la fiesta con palabras como alienación.

(La segunda recapitulación habrá que hacerla bien entrada la noche, cuando los niños estén profundamente dormidos y tú te resistas, te resistas pensando en un juego para cuando llegue la mañana y se despierten. Esta misma página servirá, como una receta, cocina del mundo. Que cuenten todas las palabras que empiecen por la letra d. Acostarlas en la playa de papel y así construir un tejado de pizarra para las próximas intemperies. Mientras ellos pintan des tú puedes preparar unas natillas o leche frita, y mientras el postre se hace aprovechar para leer unos fragmentos de la *Guía espiritual de Castilla*, de José Jiménez Lozano, o del *Robinson Crusoe*, de Daniel Defoe (Marcel Proust siempre supo que era mejor la Venecia del ensueño que la Venecia real).

El mercado de las palabras no es el de los fabricantes de máscaras, sobre todo si no empleamos los términos en su sentido literal. La d es la cuarta letra del abecedario de la luz y de la oscuridad. Guy Debord alumbra desde la muerte como John Berger alumbra desde este lado de la oscuridad. Hubiera querido escribir desde cinco dedos sentidos, pero lo que digo no es todo lo que pienso. Decir forma parte de las estratagemas del damero maldito, de los dioses fieramente humanos, de la duración de un texto como si fuera una sintonía para las noches de conducción nocturna, cuando hemos perdido el destino y la razón del viaje, acaso llueva, acaso soñemos otro texto, otra vida, otra dirección. Ese deseo que descifra signos en la noche y que pese a la decepción sigue buscando con faros que van al faro. Dar es la contraseña para la próxima frontera.

Matador, D, 1999, Spain

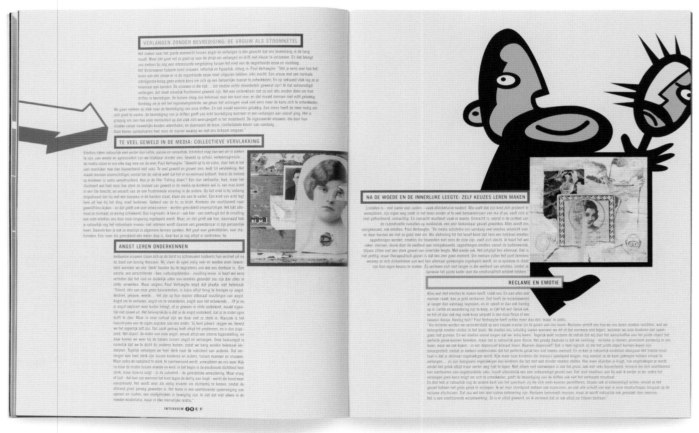

Artur, Summer 1998, Germany

marked with a black permanent marker. "Venison 1-1/2 pounds tied roast," the label might say, or "1 pound Venison steak," and then the year. I was happy for two reasons: the deer would no longer haunt my walk to the car, and dinner would be magnificent.

SOMEWHERE

along the way, though, I started to question that dinner so proudly served. I still wonder exactly what it was that started to draw me away from meat, but as much as the violence of hunting, it must have been the fact that when one is around hunting, it's impossible to disassociate meat from its origin. Meat isn't something prepackaged at the grocery store; it comes from an animal—one that, probably, we kept pictures of on our living room walls, next to pictures of loved ones.

Speak, Summer 2000, USA

Geburt und Tod (Bardo des gewöhnlichen Lebens), zwischen Einschlafen und Aufwachen (Bardo der Träume) und zwischen Tod und nächstem Leben (Bardo des Werdens). Zu jedem Zeitpunkt befindet sich der Mensch in einer oder mehreren Bardo-Situationen, vorangetrieben durch die Kraft vergangener, eigener Handlungen (Karma).Einzigartig an den sechs Yoga-Traditionen ist, dass sie eine Anzahl von meditativen Techniken anbieten, um diese drei Zustände zu erreichen .Eine besonders effektive Übung ist demnach, auch wenn das für den Laien unverständlich klingt, das Yoga des Sterbens.

o Zustand_.

OTOS **CHRISTOPHE MARGOT**

~~Entsprechend der Schriften beginnt der Tod mit einem Prozess der teilweisen Auflösung, in der Sinne und Energien, die an das Bewusstsein gekoppelt sind, stufenweise zerfallen.~~ Die Auflösungen beruhen zum Teil auf Erfahrungen aus unserem täglichen Leben, vor allen auf denen, die wir beim Einschlafen machen. Sie können von fortgeschrittenen Yoga-Schülern durch Meditation bewusst herbeigeführt werden. Aber nur im Moment des Todes erfährt man sie ganz und unausweichlich. Wenn Übende ihre Fähigkeiten in dieser Hinsicht verfeinern, lernen sie auch, diese Techniken im Schlaf herbeizuführen. Das soll den Vorteil haben, dass der Tod für derart Ausgebildete jeden Schrecken verliert. Für sie ist der Tod, als „würde ein Säugling in den Mutterleib zurückkehren", wie es in Tibet heißt.
Um es also einmal ganz profan auf den Punkt zu bringen: Die Ausbildung in Yoga ist so etwas wie eine Führerscheinprüfung für den post-mortalen Raum. Denn nur der Yogafan ist im Moment des Todes in der Lage, sich überhaupt aus dem Kreislauf aus Geburt und Tod zu befreien. Und nur er ist dank seiner Meditationen mit der Situation vertraut.

Adrenalin, No. 6, 2001, Germany

---

too. He likes well-turned wood like these columns with their raked angles and soft edges, so beautifully mitered and dovetailed and especially pleasing because of the way they butt up against metal. It gives you the pleasure of the unexpected, putting familiar things in new contexts.

Pleasure,
Surprise,
Comfort,
Entertain,

these are the important words in the book Rizzoli is putting out about him, the carrots he followed out of nowhere to run an eighty-person firm that designed the new Academy Awards theater (the one with the goofy facade, the five-story theater curtain pulled to one side) and the billion-dollar Mohegan Sun casino and the new headquarters for advertising firm McCann-Erickson and the new children's hospital in the Bronx—the guy the City of New York approached to design the viewing platforms for the site of the former World Trade Center. In a field deeply rooted in

Esquire, March 2002, USA

---

nce upon a time, women didn't swear. Women didn't soil their dainty mouths with expletives. There was no need. They used gentle words to get their womanly point across. Women weren't women back then – they were ladies. They wore hats. And in place of swearing, they would cry, 'Oh sugar!' Even while giving birth. Those days are long gone, of course. Madonna scandalised America by saying 'fuck' during an appearance on David Letterman's late-night chat show in 1994. Not only did she say 'fuck', she said it 14 times. Someone actually bothered to count. If Madonna had been a man, no one would have even cared.

'A GIRL WHO SAYS, "PASS ME THE FUCKIN' SALT," "PASS ME THE FUCKIN' SALAD," "PASS ME THE FUCKIN' WINE," AND THEN SAYS, "LET'S GO FUCK" – BY THAT TIME, WHO WANTS TO?' BURT REYNOLDS

When it comes to women and cursing, hypocrisy is alive and well. It's OK for rap artists of both sexes to rhyme obscenity after obscenity. It's expected of professional wrestlers to have mouths so filthy they can't kiss their mothers. Surgeons must swear blue streaks during surgery. Porters can't ask for a cuppa without a few choice words thrown in. As for soldiers, well – we all know what they say about troopers. But let one woman slip up with a tiny, 'Fuck a duck!' and formerly normal people mutate into righteous jerks.
In a recent survey conducted by NOP on foul language, 70 per cent of women said that profanity was more shocking when uttered by a woman. If that woman is a mum, the sin is even worse. Many of us vividly recall the first time we heard our mothers swear. For many of us, this was the first time we realised mum was actually human. 'She was middle-class, Guardian-reading and she said, "Oh, fuck," and I was stunned,' says a friend of the time her best friend's mum cursed out loud. 'My mother has never said that word. It was as if her mum had come downstairs naked and reeking of gin and said, "OK, who wants me first?"'
Swearing is a manly thing – so manly that a swearing woman turns the world upside down. Julia Roberts' character in Erin Brockovich was considered low-class because of her bulging breasts, but ultimately unstoppable because she swore like a man. Of course, some women think swearing makes us just

Men swear more often, it's true. But after studying words of British English conversations, Dr Tony M multilingual corpus linguistics at Leicester Unive that while men swear more than women, woman a slouches 'Women,' he says, 'actually swear pretty And they don't shy away from particular types of such as "Fuck you" or general imprecations such
Women will catch up with men in the swearing that's for sure. Swearing is too natural, fun and we Besides, the reasons for us not to swear are slowly world isn't 'ladylike' these days. If women aren't with a stream of expletives, we'll have to take the and demand fucking verbal equality. Men, like the yelp as they please. They can also pee outside, bo As we can't do one, we'll do the other.
Anyway, it turns out that swearing is good for yo normal way to express emotions,' says Dr Timothy psychology at Massachusetts College of Liberal Ar don't swear is saying that they don't have any emo your car. It's built into us.' It's so natural, in fact, th they know which side of the brain – the right – is r at blue. Patients with damage to the left side cann but they don't lose the ability to swap eloquently a
Everyone – man, woman and child – is swearing today. There is no mystery as to why. As comic Pro up: 'Things are more irritating than ever.' Women c not more daily stress than men. That's why, when themselves, swearing is such a release. Women c to shock, to vent, to warn interlopers that they

'THE DOG WHIMPERS IN ITS SLEEP; IT'S HAVI SO AM I. IT'S CALLED LIVING IN FUCKING BRI

Mostly though, women swear because swearing swearing among friends is the accepted – and othe

Nova, No. 9, 2000, Great Britain

---

than-life. Dat is voorbij. De kijkers hebben wel door hoe reclame mand kijkt meer naar een Martini-reclame en denkt: "Als ik Martini waan ik me op een paradijselijk strand." Het is gewoon maar een Mooie vrouwen, lekker rennen, een kokosnoot die breekt, het is lac geworden.'

==
2. Humor in een postmoderne wereld

Want in een postmoderne wereld kijken we door de signalen heen willen laten kopen. We weten dat men op ons geld uit is, laat die op z'n minst leuk zijn.
'Ja, reclame ontwikkelt zich steeds meer in de richting van entertai je *Shots* [Engels videomagazine met commercials, red.] bekijkt, allemaal geestig.'
Daar win je je prijzen mee.
'Of met schoonheid. Ik ken een Braziliaanse commercial van een een meisje die samen zitten te eten. Het meisje ziet er goed uit: ten, alles. De jongen is breed en heeft een volle haardos. Die twee discussie in de trant van: zou je nog van me houden als ik niet zo'n dervlekje had? Ja, zegt die jongen. Haalt het meisje die moedervle gezicht. En zou je nog van me houden als... Die borsten blijken zijn pruik af, verwijdert z'n schoudervullingen. Heel mooi gearmd lo eindelijk weg. De pay-off is dan zoiets als: dit drankje is puur ook

Credits, No. 1, 2000, Netherlands

---

us paragon of o than with nic super- he album ent experi- track: "Race multi-tracked ecay, disease, the edge of acy and the Lots and lots

omp comes erspective stances: ssist Michael d drummer poisonous e creepy tion of the he new s like "A Light," and

only the performers—at the same time, we're also the technicians. That really is our identity now, to be the technicians of this emotion, instead of there being guys who cry into the microphone and the guys in the white coats make it all work. We're occupying both roles at the same time. The idea of being an explorer, of being a curious guy, I want that to be part of it, because we're always complaining about how things are, and how we could change the world."

"STILL THE LAST VOLUNTEER BATTLES ON. . ."

The Flaming Lips saga, and their journey from the transgressive to the transcendent, goes back to 1983, when Coyne, brother Mark, Ivins, and the forgotten first in a long line of drummers gigged at an Oklahoma City transvestite bar called the Blue Note. What made the Lips stand out from the hardcore pack was that their Oklahoma punk rock was filtered through classic icons like Zep, Floyd and the Who, resulting in such brain-bursting albums as 1987's sophomore outing, Oh

Raygun, August 1999, USA

TYPOGRAPHY.Quotes

A second level of information within the text

Like the free-standing subheading, quotes function as a means of breaking up the text in order to make it more accessible. They can be direct quotations, or they can be in the form of short summaries. In both cases, they create a second level of information which should be designed in such a manner that it stands out from the rest of the text and gives the reader a new impetus. There are lots of formal variations possible – a different font from that of the main text, other typographical distinctions, and even the possibility of combining the quote with photos and coloured areas.

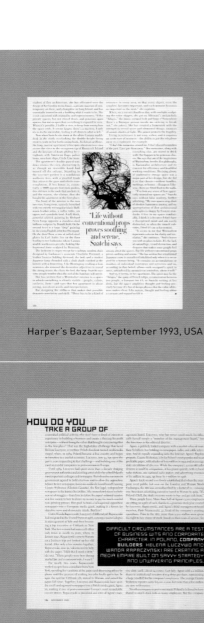

Harper's Bazaar, September 1993, USA

Fast Company, No. 11, 2000, Great Britain

Esquire, September 2001, USA

Dazed & Confused, March 2002, USA

Harper's Bazaar, October 1993, USA

Mixt(e), No. 8, 2000, France

"I want a comfortable place filled with things we love," explains Carolyn of their landmarked 12,000-square-foot work-in-progress on Gramercy Park.

Harper's Bazaar, June 1995, USA

While Celera stole headlines claiming to have cracked the human genome, Incyte makes it possible to put the knowledge to use.

Wired, June 2002, USA

Black Book, June/July/August 2000, Great Britain

Rolling Stone, December 2000, USA

Rolling Stone, December 2000, USA

Rolling Stone, June 2000, USA

Harper's Bazaar, December 1993, USA

cluding 408 homicides. About ten percent of all the city's gang crimes were occurring in the Rampart Division, eight square miles of decaying apartment buildings and scabrous storefronts located between Hollywood and downtown. Rampart neighborhoods were the most densely populated in Los Angeles, home to perhaps the highest percentage of illegal immigrants in the state. Vendors who peddled oranges and rock cocaine worked side by side, while nannies and gardeners who sent half their paychecks back home waited for buses along the perimeter of McArthur Park, which had become probably the largest open-air drug market in the U.S.

Most of that drug trade was controlled by the Eighteenth Street Gang, by far the city's biggest, with as many as 20,000 members scattered in subgroups, or "cliques," up and down the West Coast, from Tijuana, Mexico, to Portland, Oregon. The gang wove together layers of criminal enterprise that used a system of "tax" collection to link drug trafficking all the way from the powerful, prison-based Mexican mafia at the top to the small-time independent dealers at the bottom. More than 150 murders were tied to the Eighteenth Street Gang between 1985 and 1995. Residents all across the city, and especially in the neighborhoods most affected, wanted the gang dealt with.

In this context, joining CRASH during the mid-1990s was more like becoming a Special Forces fighter in a wartime army than anything resembling traditional police work. An officer's performance was judged almost entirely by how many gangsters he put behind bars. Rampart's CRASH team not only had its own logo – the aces and eights of Wild Bill Hickock's Dead Man's Hand – but even its own headquarters in a detective substation a mile from the main division station. WE INTIMIDATE THOSE WHO INTIMIDATE OTHERS, read the motto above the front entrance. Officers worked mostly at night and without any real supervision. If an officer made arrests that led to convictions, he was doing a good job; if not, he lacked the "initiative" that anti-gang work required.

Ray Perez had been a top "producer" as an undercover narcotics cop and continued to make a high number of arrests on the Rampart CRASH unit. And perhaps no other detective on the LAPD could match his effectiveness as a witness in court. Public defender Tamar Toister recalls feeling helpless as she watched Perez testify against her client Javier Ovando in early 1997. Toister figured that both judge and jury might feel sympathy for her client. Perez and his partner, Nino Durden, shot Ovando three times in the process of arresting him, and the nineteen-year-old was left paralyzed from the waist down. Ovando had to be wheeled into court on a gurney at his preliminary hearing and would be confined to a wheelchair for the rest of his life.

But after Perez described how Ovando (whose gang name was Sniper) had attempted to ambush him and his partner with an assault rifle, Ovando's fate was sealed. "He was better on the witness stand," Toister says, "than any police officer I've ever cross-examined: smooth, sincere, articulate, with just the right amount of emotion." Duly impressed, Judge Stephen Czuleger sentenced Ovando to twenty-three years in state prison – even more time than the prosecutor had asked for. "That was entirely due to how good Perez had been on the stand," Toister says. "I have to admit, I believed him myself."

Perez's career probably would be thriving still if Poole hadn't started looking into the detective's involvement with Mack at almost exactly the same time a clerk in the LAPD's Property Division discovered that more than six pounds of pure cocaine had been either lost or stolen. Even then, only Perez's bad luck permitted the LAPD to tie him to the missing coke. The dope had been signed out on March 2nd, 1998, to LAPD officer Joel Perez, who was startled by an April notice asking him to return it to the Property Division. He hadn't checked out any three kilos of coke, Joel Perez said. Shown a sign-out sheet bearing his name and badge number, the officer insisted it was a forgery. The property officer who had released the coke, Laura Castellanos, said she didn't remember ever seeing Joel but did recall handing over a carton of narcotics to an Officer Ray Perez.

RAFAEL PEREZ *gave testimony that exposed the Rampart scandal but cut short the bigger case.*

Facing jail time for theft, Perez gave prosecutors a statement that implicated more than seventy of his fellow officers. He said that in one incident, a gang member was used as a human battering ram until his head punched through a wall; in another, a man was hung from a fire escape by his ankles until he talked.

Once detectives put Ray under surveillance, they began to wonder just how large a criminal conspiracy they were dealing with. "Perez and Durden and Sammy Martin were meeting for lunch every day," Poole says. "Then they'd reconnoiter in the middle of the night behind a urinal stall in Griffith Park."

By late spring of 1998, Perez was the target of a specially formed LAPD unit. Today it is called the Rampart Task Force, but back then it was known simply as the Robbery-Homicide Task Force, and its creation was almost entirely a response to the detective work of Poole. "The connections that Russ Poole had made between the David Mack bank robbery and the Biggie Smalls murder, including the possibility that LAPD officers might be involved, were the origin of the task force," says Richard Rosenthal, the first prosecutor assigned to the task force by the district attorney's office. "Then you had the theft of the cocaine, and at that point, Chief Parks says, 'OK, wait. What's going on here?'"

By 1998, task-force detectives realized that Perez had for some time been taking advantage of the LAPD's absurdly loose system for checking out drugs as court evidence. Essentially, all a detective had to do was make a phone call to the Property Division, give his last name and badge number, then ask that the dope be sent to him by courier. The drugs had to be returned, of course, but the Property Division rarely checked to find out whether what they got back was pure cocaine or a bag of Bisquick.

A "close audit" of all narcotics evidence checked out during the previous six months swiftly turned up a second (and earlier) suspicious transfer of cocaine to the Rampart Division, this one involving a pound booked into evidence by Detective Frank Lyga. Poole soon became convinced – and so did several other detectives – that Perez had targeted Lyga's coke as retaliation for the shooting of Kevin Gaines. "We all agreed this was just way too big a coincidence," says Poole.

In July 1998, while still under surveillance, Perez was photographed in a "romantic embrace" with a juicy-looking nightclub singer whom he knew as Bella Rios. Her real name was Veronica Quesada. During one surveillance operation, Poole and another detective knocked at her door at a time when they knew she would answer.

"Veronica Quesada knows English, but she wouldn't speak it to us," Poole says. "She kept saying, 'No comprendo.' She's no easy mark, I can tell you that." Frustrated, Poole began to look about the woman's living room, where he spotted a photograph of Ray Perez wearing a red sweat suit and flashing a Bloods gang sign. "I remember thinking, 'I knew it,'" Poole recalls. A moment later, Quesada's brother Carlos Romero walked into the apartment carrying a quarter-pound of cocaine. "The brother was so dumbfounded, he just stood there," Poole says. "It might have been the easiest coke bust in history."

Within a couple of weeks, detectives from the task force established numerous links between Perez, Quesada and Carlos Romero. The most significant of these was that in the past year both Quesada and Romero had been convicted of felonies for dealing cocaine, yet each had received a suspended sentence. In both cases, the judges who heard their cases received requests for leniency from Detective Ray Perez.

At the time of her arrest in April 1997, detectives learned that Quesada was in possession of "pay/owe" sheets bearing the initials "RP" and the phone number for the Rampart Division. On the date that the three kilos of cocaine were checked out of the LAPD's Property Division, supposedly by officer Joel Perez, Ray Perez had made a total of eight phone calls to Quesada and Romero. The detective made more than 160 calls to the same numbers between November 1997 and June 1998.

When questioned, Perez explained both his requests for leniency and the phone calls by claiming that Quesada was a "former informant" with whom he had, unfortunately, become sexually involved. "The guy was cool under questioning," says Poole. "But when I saw him one afternoon at the police academy, you could tell he was scared shitless. He was looking around all the time, over his shoulder and behind his back. He knew we were closing in on him."

98 · ROLLING STONE, JUNE 7, 2001

Rolling Stone, June 2001, USA

Premium, No. 3, 2001, Germany

Speak, February 2000, USA

De Doos van Pandora

_ Edith van Loo: 's lands bekendste onbekende dj

Blvd., No. 3, 2001, Netherlands

A meaningful combination of textual and pictorial information

Captions are not headings, even if some creative spirits prefer to put them above the picture. In terms of content, a caption should provide a meaningful explanation of the picture, rather than merely describing it. A popular form is the division into a factual part and a commentary, sometimes separated by a colon. In the layout, the gap between picture and caption must be clear, and the font must also be easily distinguishable from that of the main text. There's no need for the pictures themselves to conform to the layout grid. Quite often captions are actually positioned within the photo,

either by reversing them out or by overprinting. This method cannot be applied indiscriminately, but must fit in with the overall concept of the magazine. The higher the quality and information content of the picture, the more irksome will be the incorporation of a text. A carefully thought out combination of picture and text can have a definite impact on the style of a magazine. As regards the use of purely symbolic pictures, captions are superfluous, since they would actually destroy the whole purpose of the symbol.

Mare, December 2001/January 2002, Germany

A&W, June/July 2001, Germany

Ahead, No. 1, 2001, Austria

DFusion, March 1999, Germany

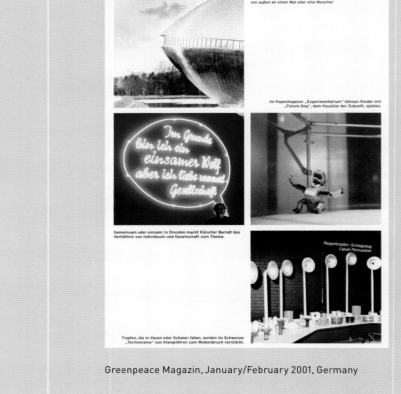

Greenpeace Magazin, January/February 2001, Germany

Big, No. 28, 2000, USA

Premium, No. 1, 2001, Germany

★ **Sterrenkok**

Erik van Loo (36, vissen) is chef-kok van restaurant de Zwetheul in
Zweth, dat tussen Rotterdam en Delft ligt. Hij heeft een Michelin-
ster. Al jaren.

"We hebben hier nu sinds 1991 een ster. Daarvoor had ik een eigen
zaak, Duurstede, ook met een ster. Daarvoor werkte ik bij De Savel-
horn ook een ster. En daarvoor hij [...] twee sterren en weer daar-

★ **Voetbalster**

Daphne Koster (19, vissen) voetbalt in het Nederland[...]
En dat maakt haar dus voetbalster en voetbalstér.

Daphne Koster (19, vissen) is centraal verdediger van
damesvoetbalelftal. Linker centraal verdedigster on[...]
want de verdediging van Oranje speelt op lijn. Op[...]

Blvd., December 2000, Netherlands

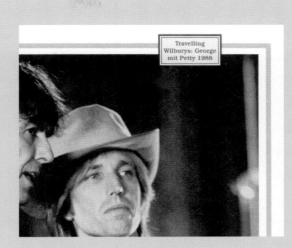

Rolling Stone, February 2002, Germany

Style, July/August 2001, Germany

AD, December 2001/January 2002, France

Raygun, March 1999, USA

Premium, No. 3, 2001, Germany

TYPOGRAPHY.Tables

A system for the quick grasp of comparable information

The function of tables is to offer the reader a clearly laid out collection of factual information. In most magazines little attention is paid to their design: tables can rarely be enhanced with graphics or illustrations as this would generally detract from their clarity and accessibility. Even so, within these restricted parameters it's still possible to make their design attractive. In addition to purely typographical means, good use can be made of lines and spaces. In choosing the font, it's important to ensure that single-spaced tabular numerals are used, as the different sets of numbers and decimal points must stand directly below one another. Old-style numerals are generally inappropriate for this function, and because of their long ascenders and descenders tend to look very messy.

Vogue Pelle, No. 7, 2001, Italy

Mac Magazin, No. 3, 2000, Germany

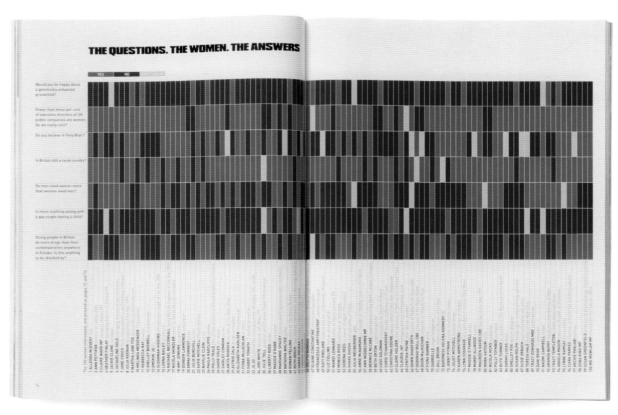

Nova, No. 6, 2000, Great Britain

Whitening

SOMETIMES A GENTLER CLEANING IS ALL THAT'S NEEDED. TRY THE mildest cleanser, the first one mentioned below, then work your way up. Always test any new product in a hidden spot.

MATERIAL	CLEANSERS	APPLICATIONS
CANVAS *tennis shoes*	Laundry detergent, powder or liquid; Lemon juice	Sturdy canvas tennis shoes can be machine-laundered. For extra brightening, add lemon juice to the final rinse cycle, then let shoes dry in the sunlight.
CERAMICS *teacups, coffee cups*	Denture tablets	Fill cup with warm water, add tablet, and wait until the fizzing stops. Empty the cup when water is clear. Repeat until all traces of stain are gone. For whitening aged, dingy ceramics, see "Earthenware," below.
CONCRETE *garage floors, sidewalks*	Powdered laundry detergent	Wet concrete, then sprinkle detergent over stains, and scrub with a hard-bristled brush. Rinse well. For oil stains, first soak up oil with an absorbent, such as cat litter, then sweep away, and wash.
CORIAN *countertops and other hard synthetic surfaces*	Abrasive cleanser, such as Comet; Steel wool (without cleanser)	These synthetic surfaces are extremely durable and can stand up to scrubbing. Use abrasive cleanser on a damp sponge, and rinse. For stubborn stains, scrub with a fine-grade steel wool.
DELICATE FABRICS *linens, lace*	Mild laundry detergent, such as Ivory Flakes; Oxygen bleach; Chlorine bleach (as last resort)	Hand-launder with mild detergent. If still dingy, soak in ½ cup oxygen bleach to 2 gallons water. Treat tough stains on sturdy fabrics with a weak chlorine-bleach solution: 1 teaspoon per gallon of water to start.
EARTHENWARE *white ironstone, unpainted china*	Hydrogen peroxide, commercial grade if available; Chlorine bleach (as last resort)	In a covered plastic container, soak in hydrogen peroxide up to 3 days; check often. For worse stains, use half chlorine bleach, half distilled water, up to 3 days. Follow with soaking in distilled water.
GROUT *bathroom tile*	Baking soda; Chlorine bleach	Wet grout, and apply baking soda with a small scrub brush, working quickly so that soda doesn't dissolve and lose abrasiveness. Rinse well. If necessary, spot-treat stubborn mildew with diluted chlorine bleach.
IVORY *piano keys*	Warm water; Liquid dishwashing soap, such as Ivory	Wipe each piano key with cheesecloth dampened with warm water. If necessary, use a drop of mild soap, then wipe again with a clean damp cloth. Badly stained ivory should be buffed by a professional.
LAMINATES *Formica countertops*	Liquid dishwashing soap, such as Ivory; Baking soda; Chlorine bleach	Follow manufacturer's instructions. Clean with a damp sponge and mild soap; rinse. Treat stains with a paste of baking soda and water, then rinse well. Use diluted chlorine bleach for tough stains; test first.
LEATHER AND SUEDE *upholstery, shoes*	Leather cleaner or saddle soap; Lemon juice	Whiten leather upholstery with saddle soap or leather cleaner; let dry; repeat if necessary. For white suede shoes, remove surface dirt with a stiff-bristled brush, then rub with lemon juice, and leave in sun to dry.
PAINTED SURFACES *walls*	Pine oil cleanser; Mild bleaching cleanser, such as Soft Scrub with Bleach	Wipe down walls with damp sponge periodically; for a more thorough cleaning, use pine-oil cleanser diluted in a bucket of water. If necessary, spot-treat stains with a dab of Soft Scrub with Bleach, and rinse.
PORCELAIN *sinks, bathtubs*	Liquid dishwashing soap, such as Ivory; Baking soda; Mild abrasive cleanser, such as Soft Scrub	Clean regularly with warm water and mild soap. For stains, use a mild abrasive such as baking soda or Soft Scrub on a damp sponge, and rinse well. Avoid harsh abrasives, which can scratch or dull the surface.
RUBBER AND HARD PLASTIC *spatulas, cutting boards*	Liquid dishwashing soap, such as Ivory; Chlorine bleach	Wash utensils in hot, soapy water after contact with staining foods. Whiten and remove stubborn stains by soaking in a 50 percent chlorine bleach and water solution for an hour, checking periodically. Rinse well.
STONE *marble floors, countertops*	Liquid dishwashing soap, such as Ivory; Vinegar; Marble cleaner, such as Marble Magic	Some polished marble can be damaged by anything harsher than warm water, so follow manufacturer's instructions. For soap scum in showers, try a diluted mixture of vinegar and water; rinse well.

108

Living, No. 5, 2000, Great Britain

Wachstumsfirmen enttäuschen

Die 20 besten Geschäftsberichte der Nemax-50-Unternehmen (Maximale Punktzahl: 100)

Rang	Unternehmen	Inhalt	Finanz-kommunikation	Optik	Sprache	Gesamt*	Urteil**
1	EM.TV	56,90	60,00	64,57	78,33	65,56	gut
2	Brokat	54,38	51,00	66,89	59,16	59,91	befriedigend
3	Intershop	50,30	52,00	51,98	82,91	59,76	befriedigend
4	Heyde	48,38	55,00	50,82	85,00	55,25	befriedigend
5	SER Systeme	54,38	57,00	38,63	69,58	54,69	befriedigend
6	Mobilcom	50,36	46,00	50,05	79,58	54,04	befriedigend
7	Pfeifer Vacuum	46,13	55,50	48,89	82,50	53,40	befriedigend
8	Kinowelt	50,35	45,50	36,50	65,83	49,87	ausreichend
9	SCM Microsystems	39,51	41,00	59,15	85,41	49,56	ausreichend
10	Edel Music	39,45	46,00	53,34	81,66	48,88	ausreichend
11	1&1	46,82	47,00	34,17	71,25	48,62	ausreichend
12	mb Software	40,72	40,50	50,44	83,33	48,54	ausreichend
13	ce Consumer Electronic	43,37	41,00	50,82	71,66	48,38	ausreichend
14	Infomatec	42,84	48,50	43,85	60,16	47,78	ausreichend
15	Qiagen	44,86	41,00	26,43	77,08	46,35	ausreichend
16	Aixtron	42,08	43,50	27,01	75,41	45,03	ausreichend
17	Micrologica	39,52	36,50	52,57	65,83	44,97	ausreichend
18	Singulus	39,98	43,50	40,37	64,16	44,19	ausreichend
19	Ixos	36,46	42,00	43,85	73,33	43,93	ausreichend
20	Teldafax	37,49	41,00	37,85	67,91	42,64	ausreichend

*Setzt sich zusammen aus den Ergebnissen in den vier Beurteilungskategorien sowie dem abschließenden Urteil der Jury. **Schulnotensystem: Ab 75 Punkte: sehr gut, von 74,99 bis 62,50: gut, von 62,49 bis 50,00: befriedigend, von 49,99 bis 37,50: ausreichend, weniger als 37,50: mangelhaft.

Newcomer bieten viel Durchschnitt

Die 20 besten Geschäftsberichte der Börsenneulinge (Maximale Punktzahl: 100)

Rang	Unternehmen	Inhalt	Finanz-kommunikation	Optik	Sprache	Gesamt*	Urteil**
1	Celanese	55,50	67,00	57,02	79,58	65,77	gut
2	Stinnes	55,79	60,50	54,50	82,08	64,10	gut
3	Edscha	54,80	54,00	59,54	87,08	63,79	gut
4	Vivanco	55,74	56,00	57,02	77,50	59,24	befriedigend
5	Epcos	56,15	62,00	50,05	74,16	58,81	befriedigend
6	Elexis	55,69	55,50	48,50	76,25	57,67	befriedigend
7	Schuler	51,32	57,50	48,69	75,58	55,49	befriedigend
8	BinTec Communications	51,37	47,00	56,44	75,83	55,14	befriedigend
9	Adcon Telemetry	55,56	50,00	37,85	73,75	54,80	befriedigend
10	Adva Optical	52,47	49,50	45,98	72,91	54,12	befriedigend
11	MVV Energie	52,56	54,00	44,43	69,58	54,11	befriedigend
12	CyBio	52,09	47,00	38,04	82,50	53,78	befriedigend
13	Agfa-Gevaert	51,96	48,50	46,95	69,16	53,27	befriedigend
14	ADS	53,51	50,00	31,46	74,58	52,84	befriedigend
15	CPU Softwarehouse	52,45	46,00	40,76	71,25	52,55	befriedigend
16	AT&S Austria Technologies	51,56	53,00	31,66	75,00	52,31	befriedigend
17	Zapf Creation	48,96	46,50	46,95	73,75	52,01	befriedigend
18	Beate Uhse	50,57	51,50	37,66	69,16	51,56	befriedigend
19	PC-Spezialist	53,51	58,50	27,20	63,33	51,23	befriedigend
20	Easy Software	49,00	50,00	40,56	67,08	50,60	befriedigend

*Setzt sich zusammen aus den Ergebnissen in den vier Beurteilungskategorien sowie dem abschließenden Urteil der Jury. **Schulnotensystem: Ab 75 Punkte: sehr gut, von 74,99 bis 62,50: gut, von 62,49 bis 50,00: befriedigend, von 49,99 bis 37,50: ausreichend, weniger als 37,50: mangelhaft.

Manager Magazin, No. 10, 2000, Germany

111111111

111111111

Martha Stewart Living, March 2002, USA

Anleger, No. 3, 2001, Germany

Wired, July 2001, USA

Wired, June 2000, USA

Three basic forms and their illustrative permutations

Charts are mainly used in business and financial magazines, and can basically be divided into three types. First, the pie chart, which starts out whole (i.e. 100%) and is then cut up into larger or smaller pieces. Dynamic developments cannot be traced with this form, only the status quo. The second form is the bar chart, which compares sizes and quantities in precise figures, but cannot effectively display percentages. Graphically, the representation can range from two-dimensional figures to round or rectangular columns, sometimes combined with different structures or shades. The third type is the graph, with systems of coordinates that can show developments over time. This is most commonly used to show the progress of items like shares. Since one chart may often contain several graphs, sometimes intersecting, the use of structures or shades can be a hindrance. As always, the main consideration has to be clarity, precision of layout, and instant grasp of the facts.

Wired, April 2002, USA

Pie chart

Bar chart

Graph

Style, November 2001, Germany

Fast Company, March 2000, USA

Wired, February 2000, USA

Wired, November 2000, USA

Wired, December 2000, USA

Wired, April 2000, USA

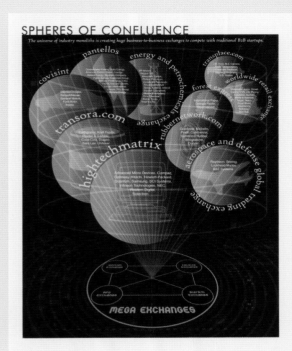

Red Herring, August 2000, USA

Wired, July 2001, USA

Wired, June 2000, USA

Manager Magazin, October 2000, Germany

Brand eins, December 1999/January 2000, Germany

Displaying information to supplement the main text

Texts which enrich an article with additional information (appendages, extracts, summaries, and so on) are often laid out in separate boxes. Even interviews that accompany the main article can be separated in the same way, creating an additional textual level.

It's important that the article itself is long enough to accommodate the extra information, and there's sometimes the danger in specialist magazines of overloading articles with boxes. In such situations, it's

sensible to provide a summary of all the additions within the layout system.

There are no formal restrictions for boxes – they can be combined with photos, illustrations, lines and coloured areas. The font should be clearly distinguishable from the one used in the main text, and generally a sans serif type is preferable. If the box is narrow, it's best to use unjustified type rather than justified.

Red Herring, January 2001, Great Britain

Fast Company, October 2000, USA

Wired, June 2000, USA

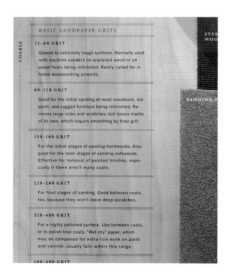

Martha Stewart Living, April 2000, USA

Fast Company, No. 11, 2000, Great Britain

Vanity Fair, No. 6, 2002, Great Britain

The Face, No. 5, 2002, Great Britain

INFOGRAPHICS

Maps, cross-sections and three-dimensional diagrams

Information graphics are used to present complex
information or scenes that cannot be directly seen,
perhaps because they are microscopically small or
geographically huge, or take place within the centre
of the earth. They can also be used for complex interior
layouts that can only be understood if we remove
the roof or a wall to get an overview of how different
spaces fit together.

Wallpaper, No. 12, 2000, Great Britain

In Graphics is the first magazine to specialize in infographics, and its first issue was published in December 2010. The editor-in-chief is Jan Schwochow, who says: 'In this magazine, the purpose is not to focus on information graphics for their own sake, but to use them to tackle contemporary topics that we find particularly interesting and want to understand.'

Where the editor meets the reader

The editorial is the editor's means of greeting the reader. It's usually situated on page three, but in magazines that start off with a collection of ads, it will be on the first page of text. There are some cases where the editorial is on the same page as the list of contents, and others where it's combined with a half-page ad. A common component is a picture of the editor plus his or her signature, but there are also purely typographical presentations without a picture. That usually depends on the nature of the editorial itself.

Here are a few different forms:
• The leader: the personal opinion of the editor
• The presentation: a survey of the contents, introducing important topics, sometimes even accompanied by pictures.
• The behind-the-scenes: background information on how individual contributions came to be written.
• The diary.
The editorial is generally the last item to be written, and it's often only finished just before the deadline.

Letter from the Publisher

In a recent speech, Cardinal Basil Hume, spiritual head of Britain's four million Catholics, criticised society's 'twin obsessions with sex and shopping' and 'the lack of spiritual qualities.' He said: 'An alien would be right to wonder for what kind of Gods we were erecting our shopping centres.'
A heavy indictment indeed. But the Cardinal was judging society by the standards of the Eighties. Although society might still be enjoying the twin thrills of sex and shopping, there is change in the air. On the cusp of the millennium, we live in a less hard-edged world, where lifestyles are increasingly tinged by feelings of responsibility and a healthy dose of common sense towards the business of living. The new consumer is a mature creature, recognising the increasing urgency to think Green, to re-assess our attitudes to the environment, to re-appreciate our great cities. Coupled with this, there is a groundswell of people 'getting in touch with themselves' – a recognition that the sensual and the soulful are as important as the sexual and the materialistic.
Are we at Viewpoint being optimistic? Well, yes, but we believe we have reason to be. The new consumer realises that it makes sense to buy less and to buy better, and understands that self-reliance and self-sufficiency are the key ingredients for future survival – together with a re-affirmation of the importance of family bonds. Welcome to the fourth edition of Viewpoint, where we analyse in detail the trend towards 'responsible' consumerism and its implications for us all. The word of the moment is 'respect' – for ourselves, for those around us and for the world we live in.

david s. fra

David Shah – Publisher

Viewpoint, September 1998, Netherlands

Vogue Nippon, No. 2, 2002, Japan

editorial　　　　编者的話

Substance, January/February 2001, Singapore

LEADER

Don't criminalize cloning research.

THE CRUSADE to criminalize human cloning, motivated by the desire not to start down the slippery slope to eugenics, will inflict substantial collateral damage to potentially life-saving therapeutic cloning of stem cells for use in cell regeneration. Numerous proposed federal and state bills in the United States would "stop the cloning process at the beginning" (in the words of one such bill) by banning even the most rudimentary experimentation, like transferring DNA into an egg cell without a nucleus, that could potentially lead to cloned individuals. The federal bills, which carry penalties of up to ten years in prison, enjoy bipartisan and presidential support. They should not.

Proponents of the bills argue that permitting the cloning of human cells would make it impossible to prevent full reproductive cloning. Maybe so, but it's worth the risk. Cloning technologies might one day produce insulin-secreting islet cells that effectively treat diabetes, or nerve cells that can repair a damaged spinal cord. Who knows what other great medical advances could emerge from this promising line of scientific inquiry? Politicians think they do know, however, and have decided these advances aren't worth risking an "affront to human dignity." Patients wasting away with Parkinson's disease or congestive heart failure may disagree.

The panic over cloning feeds off of the popular fear of a brave new world, threats by the Raelian cult to clone humans, and warnings by talking heads like William Kristol, editor and publisher of the *Weekly Standard*, about the "eugenic manipulation of human nature." But brave new worlds are more often created by authoritarian rule, not by individuals making personal medical choices. You don't spare human dignity by jailing those trying to ease human suffering. ∎

Write to editorialpage@redherring.com.

AUGUST 15, 2001 · RED HERRING **21**

Red Herring, August 2001, USA

Brett, No. 8, 2000, Germany

Ausdruck, Spring 1997, Germany

Passionate, No. 1, 2001, Netherlands

édito

"Je ne suis qu'une femme, sauvage et changeante, sans vertu aucune." Nietzsche.

Numéro, No. 31, 2002, France

Mode Max, No. 7, 2002, France

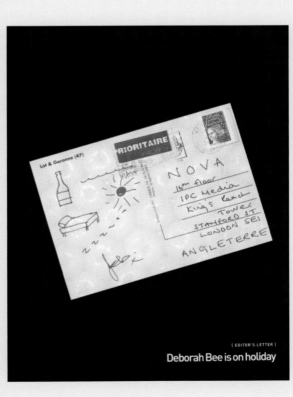

[EDITOR'S LETTER]

Deborah Bee is on holiday

Nova, No. 9, 2000, Great Britain

editor's note

Yesplease, December 2001/January 2002, Italy

TYPES OF PAGE.Contents

From a neutral list to a mouth-watering menu

There are various factors that determine the design of a list of contents. The main one is, of course, the character of the magazine itself: special interest and current affairs magazines require a different approach from that of, say, lifestyle. The form is dictated by the function. If people only read the magazine selectively, the list of contents will be different from that of a magazine that people leaf through with no particular item in mind, just waiting for something to catch their eye. In all cases, though, the list should reflect the structure of the magazine, following its sections and the order of its articles. Generally there are two levels, one pictorial and one textual, with the emphasis again depending on the nature of the magazine. Pictures may be used to emphasize certain central themes, but they also help to attract the more visually orientated reader to one particular subject. For this reason, such pictures should be supplemented with captions and page numbers. The contents page is especially attractive to advertisers, as most readers will turn to it, and lengthy lists are often spread out over two separate pages so that they can be split up by two full-page ads. For the reader, though, it's clearly easier to follow if the contents are on one page or, in really thick magazines, put together on a double-page spread. In some high-quality magazines, the list of contents is written by a journalist in order to make sure that the linguistic style is homogeneous. The page numbers themselves must be clearly laid out, either to the right or left of the subject matter; there's little room here for experimentation, because in its role as an instrument of navigation, the list's highest priorities should be clarity and ease of use.

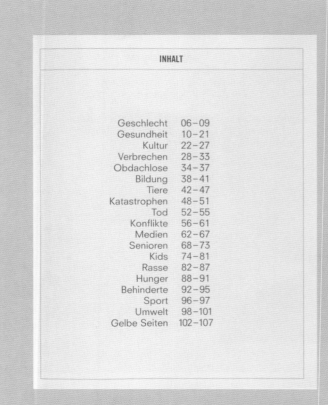

Colors, No. 46, 2001, Italy

Red Herring, No. 104, 2001, USA

Tank, No. 1, 2000, Great Britain

Speak, No. 2, 2000, USA

Eden, No. 1, 1999, Germany

Detnin Exclusief, No. 3, 2001, Netherlands

Tank, No. 4, 2001, Great Britain

Ad!dict, Spring 2001, Belgium

11 Freunde, No. 12, 2002, Germany

2wice, November 1999, USA

Tank, No. 3, 2001, Great Britain

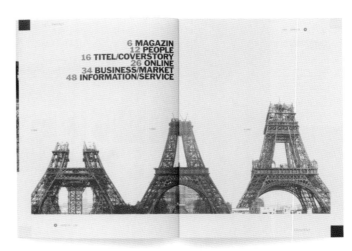

Aspects, No. 1, 2000, Germany

AM7, No. 7, 2001, Germany

Bloom, No. 5, 2000, France
Double page contents, photo by Anton Beeke

Inhalt

„Das ist mein Vorschlag: Wir vergessen jetzt einfach mal alles.
Wir vergessen den Klatsch, den Job, die vielen Leute, den ganzen Stress,
den Verkehr und all das, was wir eigentlich nicht verpassen wollten."
Peter Lau, „Nachlassenkommen"

Foto: Jens Neumann

Brand eins, No. 6, 2001, Germany

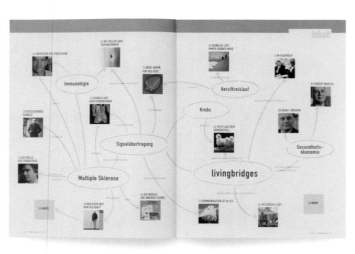

Living Bridges, No. 1, 2002, Germany

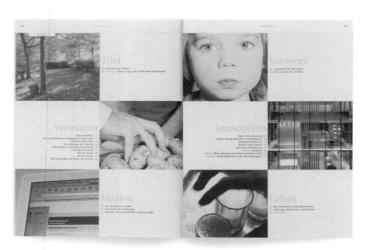

Values, No. 2, 2002, Germany

Blue Inc., 2001, Germany

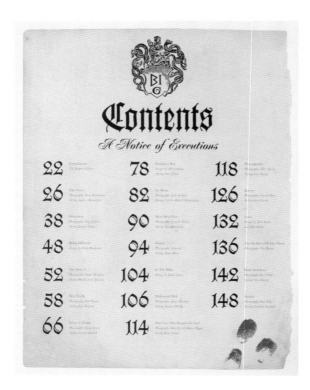

Big, No. 28, 2000, USA

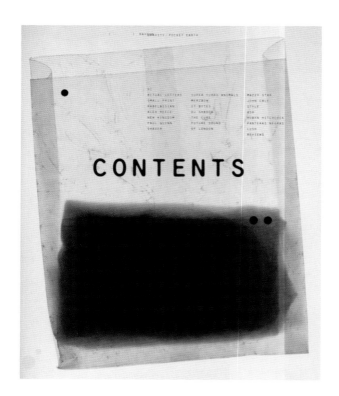

Raygun, No. 41, 1996, USA

Credits, 1999, Netherlands

Credits, No. 1, 2001, Netherlands

Credits, No. 2, 2000, Netherlands

Credits, No. 1, 2000, Netherlands

Differentiating between ads and reports

In the classic magazine, there's a strict division between ads and editorial material. Most magazines cannot survive purely on sales, and so much of the cost is borne by ads. The division should be absolutely clear to the reader – who, after all, has a right to know what interests may lie behind a particular contribution – but this isn't always the case. One official hybrid form is the advertorial – a feature written by the editorial team but paid for by a commercial client. Such contributions should really come under the umbrella of public relations, and they often actually contain offers for the reader. But there are also features that describe or recommend selected products and are written quite independently of the firms concerned. It's only when sources and prices are quoted that the article becomes a promotional exercise. When products are recommended independently, the design should ensure that the feature is easily distinguishable from an ad.

Vogue, August 2001, Great Britain

Loaded Fashion, Spring/Summer 2001, Great Britain

Bogey, June 2002, Great Britain

Home, July/August 2000, Germany

Vogue Paris, June/July 2000, France

Nova, No. 6, 2001, Germany

Ministry, August 2001, Austria

Esquire, April 2001, USA

Bare, January/February 2001, Great Britain

Mixt(e), September/October/November 2000, France

Harper's Bazaar, February 2002, USA

Ish, August 1999, Singapore

Vogue Pelle, September 2001, Italy

Ahead, No. 1, 2002, Austria

Wallpaper, July/August 2000, Great Britain

Bare, January/February 2001, Great Britain

Blond, No. 3, 2002, Germany

Snow, No. 2, 2002, Germany

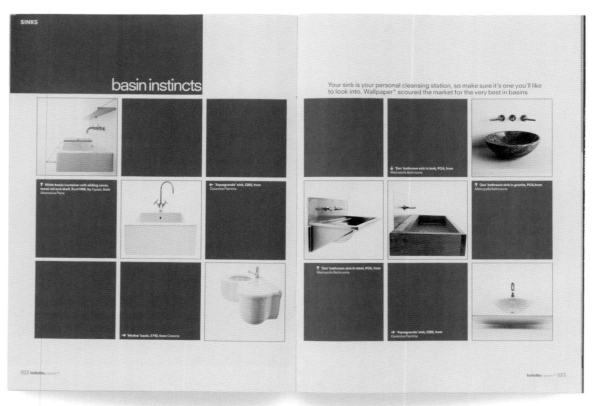

Wallpaper, No. 3, 2000, Great Britain

Room, May/July 2001, Germany

Wired, December 2000, USA

Domus, July/August 2000, Italy

Distinguishing opinion pages from the editorial

Every feature in a magazine will add up to a general reflection of editorial opinion. With political magazines it's important for the reader to know the party line that's being followed, but many magazines also pride themselves on publishing articles that express views independent of, or even contrary to, those of the editors. Such contributions, along with readers' letters, appear as comments or columns on the opinion pages.

Again, the design should make them easily recognizable, and they're often combined with a photo or drawing of the author. As well as purely textual contributions, there may be columns that lay emphasis on pictorial comparisons. The various columns and comments may be one-off or regular, and obviously the former offers more freedom to the designer than the latter.

Mixt(e), June/July/August 2001, France

Mixt(e), October/November 2001, France

Mixt(e), September/October/November 2000, France

Hemisphere, No. 1, 2001, USA

Esquire, No. 4, 2001, USA

Surface, Spring 2000, USA

The Face, No. 9, 2001, Great Britain

From publisher's name and address to full-page list of credits

A publisher's imprint is required by law. Everyone responsible for content and ads must be named, and the imprint must also contain copyright details. All other information concerning the publishers and editorial staff is for the benefit of clients and readers.

Substance, January/February 2001, Singapore

Mixt(e), No. 18, 2002, France

Cine Chart, No. 10, 2001, Germany

Material, No. 4, 2001, Switzerland

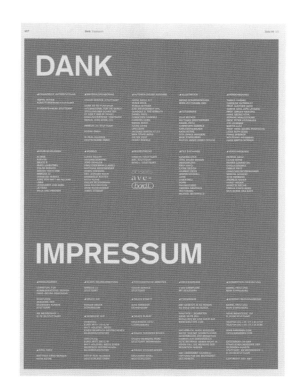

AM7, No. 7, 2001, Germany

Speak, Spring 2000, USA

Ausdruck, Spring 1997, Germany

The title pages for separate sections within a magazine

INSIDE PAGES

For all kinds of reasons, it can sometimes be necessary to make a clear distinction between different sections of the same magazine. For example, there might be extended special features which, if not published in a separate supplement, have to be integrated into the issue as a whole – a sort of magazine within a magazine. In such cases, the special features are divided off from the rest of the issue and highlighted by a title page of their own. This will, of course, be secondary to the main cover. Another optical form of division is the page that introduces a particular section. These 'pseudocovers'

are normally large-scale, with coloured areas and prominent section titles, but they can also be conceived as announcements. In fashion magazines, the first editorial page often has a dividing function – particularly in the thick, international publications that begin with fifty to a hundred pages of ads, leading eventually to the editorial section, which then proceeds uninterrupted. Fabien Baron's design for different issues of *Harper's Bazaar* consists of numerous colourful variations on the word 'Bazaar' to suit the time of year.

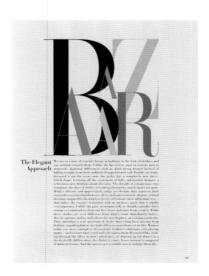

Harper's Bazaar, September 1992, USA

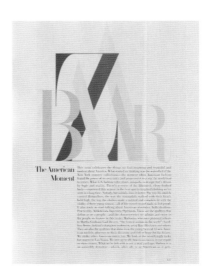

Harper's Bazaar, May 1994, USA

Harper's Bazaar, October 1992, USA

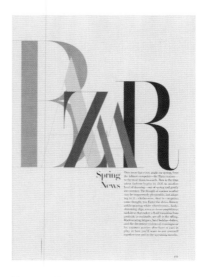

Harper's Bazaar, April 1994, USA

Harper's Bazaar, May 1998, USA

Harper's Bazaar, February 1999, USA

FUSSBALL

„Früher war ich fußball-
verrückt, aber die
ganze Entwicklung ist
zum Kotzen. Ich schaue
mir nichts mehr im
Fernsehen an, nicht mal
mehr im Radio ist es
zu ertragen. Ich gucke nur
noch Videotext ohne Ton."

1/4 nach 5, No. 4, 2002, Germany

KOSMOS

„Als er aber auf dem Wege war und
in die Nähe von Damaskus kam,
umleuchtete ihn plötzlich ein Licht
vom Himmel; und er fiel auf die
Erde und hörte eine Stimme, die
sprach zu ihm: Saul, Saul, was verfolgst du mich? Er aber sprach:
Herr, wer bist du? Der sprach: Ich
bin Jesus, den du verfolgst. Steh
auf und geh in die Stadt; da wird
man dir sagen, was du tun sollst."

1/4 nach 5, No. 4, 2002, Germany

KULTUR

Daniela Bar, BP1, Café Bedford,
Frank und Frei, Omas
Apotheke, Bar Duo: „Ist Julia hier
gewesen?" „Heute?" „Ja."
„Nein." Dschungel, Kurhaus,
Toast Bar, Die Welt ist
schön, Suryel: „Julia gesehen?"
„Nö." Café Absurd, Zoé,
Jolly Roger, Meanie Bar, Lehmitz,
Ex-Sparr: „Julia?" „Wie
wärs mit mir?"„Heute nicht."

1/4 nach 5, No. 4, 2002, Germany

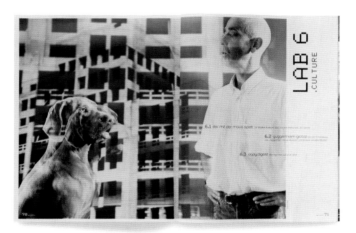

Copy, No. 10, 2001, Austria

Copy, No. 12, 2001, Austria

Börse Online, No. 4, 2002, Germany

Börse Online, No. 4, 2002, Germany

Börse Online, No. 4, 2002, Germany

Examples of dividing pages: textual introduction in *1/4 bei 5*;
large-scale double pages in *Copy*; enlarged section titles in *Börse Online*.

Original layouts from different types of magazine

The preceding chapters dealt initially with the basics of magazine design, and then with typography and the different kinds of page. This chapter looks at original, creative examples of design related to individual themes. For the most part, these themes coincide with the broad range of special interest magazines. Those of general interest have become increasingly less important; there are now so many branches of each topic that a so-called general magazine is likely to be on a single theme like music, which then splits up into fifty special interest magazines on individual aspects of the field. Whenever there are particular rules for designing these themes, they will be dealt with as they appear.

A glance at the market reveals the striking fact that there's no magazine with a monopoly on any subject. There may be market leaders, though these will change from time to time, but in countries where there's a well-developed readership for magazines, there's always lively competition. Generally each special interest section of the market creates its own visual forms so that the type of magazine will be instantly recognizable. This is particularly noticeable with computer magazines, whose covers are almost indistinguishable from one another. What they all have in common is the purely typographical list of their various topics. The assumption is that the densely packed list of subjects will be the deciding factor in the reader's choice. There seems to be no end in sight to this 'arms race', and the fact that all these magazines look like ads for supermarkets or carpet shops doesn't seem to bother the publishers. The opportunity to create a magazine with an individual identity and to steal a march on the competition appears not to enter into their calculations. The guiding principle is 'me too', and the love of conformity continues on the inside. If a magazine does dare to come up with new ideas – tests, icons, tables, sections, tips, boxes – the others will shamelessly copy them anyway. Fashion magazines are not quite so uniform. Unlike computer magazines they manage to distinguish themselves mainly through the style and standard of their photography.

Independently of style and standard, though, it's photography that moulds the design of fashion magazines. The cover already sets the tone. In women's magazines the subject is usually female, and she usually makes eye contact with the reader. Sometimes the picture is of the face only, and sometimes it's the whole body, though close-ups are more popular. Techniques of lithography and print are now so sophisticated that they can reproduce the finest details of the skin to aesthetic perfection. During the great era of the fashion magazine, the 1940s, covers were far more varied than they are today, and often made use of illustrations. As regards typography, it's a striking fact that the classical Didot with its extremely fine lines still dominates. Didot is equipped with special fonts for different sizes, and these preserve the fineness of the lines even in enlargements.

FASHION AND THE ZEITGEIST

In order to make the editorial sections of a fashion magazine distinct from the ads, the two need to be kept separate. For this reason, the major international magazines begin with a long series of ads, deliberately embracing the principle that's shunned in most other magazines – namely, to set ad next to ad. Since both sections are devoted to current fashion, this is the only way they can be kept apart. Once the editorial section is underway, a sequence of ten to twenty pages of photos per subject – with no ads in between – is ideal. The different features and reports will then be separated by

FHM, July 2001, Germany

their particular subject matter and photographic style. For instance, sequences of colour photographs may be followed by black and white, outdoor scenes by indoor, classical by experimental and so on. Ideally, the pictorial language and the formal and technical elements should all complement the content, and there should be some overall direction to the alternation of different photographic styles. Fashion photography powerfully reflects the spirit of the age, and it offers an important showcase for the world's finest photographers. The fashions depicted are often an expression of a certain way of life, as well as an extension of the formal range of pictorial language. Of course there are also many visual quotations, analogous to fashion revivals. But by and large the evolution of photography has been significantly influenced by the great fashion magazines.

The subject matter of these magazines is not, of course, restricted to fashion. It covers the whole range of modern living with themes such as make-up, health, beauty, food and drink, travel, gardening, architecture, art, the home, and so on. But on each of these subjects there are also vast numbers of special interest magazines, some elitist, some mainstream, and all adapting their visual design to the theme and to the

requirements of their own target group. This also applies to the technical composition – the paper, the type of binding, the quality of the print, and all the other refinements. The magazine's position in the market will even influence its categorisation. If it sets out to hit the mass market, it will call itself a women's rather than a fashion magazine – even if it deals with the same topics.

Its counterpart, the men's magazine, is by no means a mirror image. The main difference is the amount of space devoted to sex and erotica. In this field, the nature of the photography will vary considerably from one culture to another. Although this is perhaps something of an over-simplification, generally French erotic magazines tend to be staged voyeuristically. The man watches, the girl doesn't always know that he's watching, and so there's no eye contact. The setting is often from everyday life rather than in the artificial world of the studio, and in contrast to American magazines, for example, the focus is not always on the breasts. However, as the major men's magazines are produced under licence for a world market, for the most part there's not much difference. If you want to conquer the American market, you have to cater for American sexual predilections, and that means that in the post-*Playboy*

GQ, June 2001, Germany

Maxim, July 2001, Germany

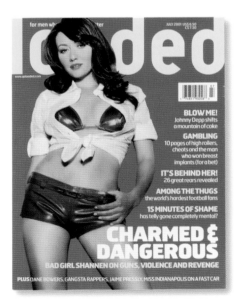

Loaded, July 2001, Great Britain

generation of magazines – *Maxim*, *FHM*, *GQ*, *Loaded* – it's the American taste that's prevailed. A concrete example of this is the collection of 2001 covers (on page 175). They all follow the same pattern: the front view of a girl in a bikini looking straight at the potential buyer. In these posed photos, the girls never quite know what to do with their hands, and so they tend to go up into their hair or down into their underwear. The background is calm and neutral – either monochrome or vaguely suggestive of a watery seaside scene. The text is in two colours (one of which is white), and the bright one is always the same as the logo. The barcode is on the right-hand side, and the only decision left to the creativity of the designer is where to put it.

PICTURE QUALITY

By comparison with other magazines that specialize in naked women, the covers mentioned above are pretty modest. Even the cover of *Playboy* is basically not all that different to some covers of the Italian *Capital*, the German *Stern*, or other picture magazines. In general the design of these magazines is greatly influenced by the quality of the picture material, and if the photos and photographers are top class, it would be a bad mistake to detract from them through clumsy use of frames, cutting, excessive text, or the addition of more photos. Here the designer must take a back seat and allow the power of the picture to speak for itself. Magazines on fashion, architecture, food, living, erotica, art, design and – for some time now – gardening as well have all become increasingly dependent on the quality of their pictures. In such publications rhythm and alternation play an essential role, giving full aesthetic value to each sequence of beautiful pictures without overdoing it. The situation is not the same with computer or business magazines, which have a different function to perform. They may require a degree of subtlety in their design, especially in the use of micro- and tabular typography, but they are not meant to catch the eye with sequences of gorgeous photos. With the relatively dry subject of business, designers will make their mark through intelligent ways of giving accessible, visual form to complex factual or abstract themes. There were plenty of good examples during the boom years at the end of the twentieth century – *Fast Company*, *Brand eins*, *Business 2.0*, *Quote*, and *Red Herring*, to name just a few.

Illustration plays a vital part here, because it can stimulate the imagination and add a personal touch that gives the feature a certain amount of colour.

TECHNOLOGY AND EMOTION

Other major players in the field are magazines on technology. Some of the most popular subjects are cars, planes, boats, bikes and cameras. There are conceptual problems here because different readers will have different interests. One group will want to focus almost exclusively on the technical side and will want immensely detailed information. The other – generally the minority – is not concerned with the technology itself, but with all the fascinating experiences connected with cars, boats, and so on, or in the case of camera enthusiasts, the main focus may be the artistic side. Some magazines strive for a compromise and combine construction with emotion. With travel magazines there are no such conflicts of interests, since the subject matter is nearly always geared to giving the reader ideas for indulging their wanderlust. The problem here is to establish a level, because there are marked differences between the potential target groups, as there are with all magazines that deal with lifestyles. What may interest the ordinary tourist may be irrelevant for the business traveller or adventurer, and vice versa. The designer must be able to use visual means in order to depict these different worlds convincingly and appropriately. The overall design of the magazine has to create a visual atmosphere individually tailored to each facet, so that the level can be identified before the reader turns to the text. When the content of a magazine is restricted to a single subject – gourmet food, for example – there's always a danger of monotony. In this case it would be a good idea not to automatically end every article with a photo of the finished dish, but to look for ways of varying the presentation. The chef at work could be shown, for instance, or the ingredients in their raw state. Food photography can also make use of different perspectives – diners seen from an angle, a meal seen from above. The essence of variety is close attention to detail.

REPORTAGE AND PORTRAITS

During the last few decades, photojournalism has undergone a major transformation. As a primary means of conveying information, it has disappeared almost totally into the background. Gone are the days of the great photo-reportages like the coronation of Queen Elizabeth II in the 1950s, when *Life* magazine rented extra accommodation in order to take photographs from all the different angles, and even chartered a plane to get the pictures back to head office as quickly as possible. Such reports clearly followed cinematic technique, using sequences of stills, but not long afterwards this kind of operation was made redundant by the mass medium of moving pictures in the form of global television. We now expect to receive our pictures live and instant. The magazine *Life* has disappeared, along with most other illustrated magazines on current affairs. War reporting as a branch of photojournalism has managed to survive, but only because there are still a few daredevil photographers who are prepared to venture deeper into the danger zones than some camera teams. Photojournalism has therefore had to change direction and seek out other subjects. This is clear from the various competitions. Photographers with artistic ambitions pick their own themes, and imprint them with their own personality. Magazines are no longer an adequate showplace for such work, and so it's often collected together and published in the more appropriate form of books. And then the magazines in turn report on the books. Meanwhile, the techniques of photojournalism have inspired other branches such as fashion and sports photography. Some photo magazines do include reports as part of a complete portfolio, but of course in this form they lose their immediacy and function only as exhibition pieces.

Portraits are an important branch of photography. It would be very unusual for a magazine, regardless of its subject matter, to appear without a portrait, no matter what the context. There is therefore a constant demand and supply. Still, you have to look long and hard for a really good specimen, as the majority of these pictures are not specially commissioned but in most cases are taken from archives. Many of them are utterly mediocre and are not worthy of closer attention. Even ambitious photographers often suffer from the lack of time available because their star subjects are too busy. No doubt there are some excellent portraits taken even when time is short, but for the most part it's impossible for a photographer to capture the essence of someone's character in a ten-minute or even thirty-minute session, while in turn the subject cannot break free from the pressures of the engagement calendar and relax sufficiently to reveal the person beneath. Most of these sessions will end in some kind of cliché pose, with the subject pretending to be hard at work, or leaning casually somewhere in the glass entrance hall of their company. Stars from the art, music or film world are usually more at ease with photographers than people from other fields, but still you can rarely glimpse anything beyond their superficial, professional poses. To increase the chances of getting a really top quality portrait, you need plenty of time, an open approach, sensitivity, and a sharp eye.

total white

PHOTOS CHRIS CRAYMER

Riscoprire il bianco. Bianco latte, gesso, ghiaccio, neve, carta, panna, burro, marmo. Puro come un giglio, delicato come un angelo, morbido come un fiocco di lana, romantico come una sposa, semplice come un uovo, scultoreo come un capitello greco. Spirituale, sofisticato, emblematico, assoluto, concettuale, essenziale, simbolico. Conservatore o trasgressivo, aristocratico o esistenzialista, sontuoso o minimale, trendy o neoclassico. Inedito protagonista di un inverno che rivaluta il candore come catarsi da un'ebbrezza multicolore.

Vogue Pelle, July 2001, Italy

Style, No. 1, 2001, Germany

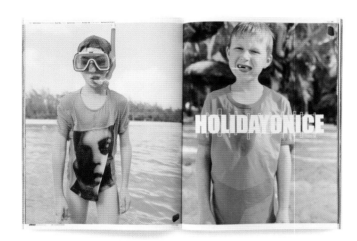

'Holiday on Ice'. Photo sequence by Astrid Grosser for *Style*.

Style, March 2001, Germany

'He wants to wear'. Fashion sequence by Claude Closky for *Big*.
These are simply portraits of models – what they want to wear
is described in the captions.

Big, No. 38, 2001, USA

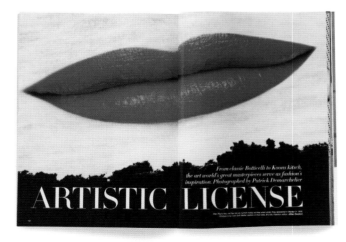

'Artistic License' – from Botticelli to Koons.
Patrick Demarchelier translates art into fashion for *Harper's Bazaar*.

Harper's Bazaar, February 2002, USA

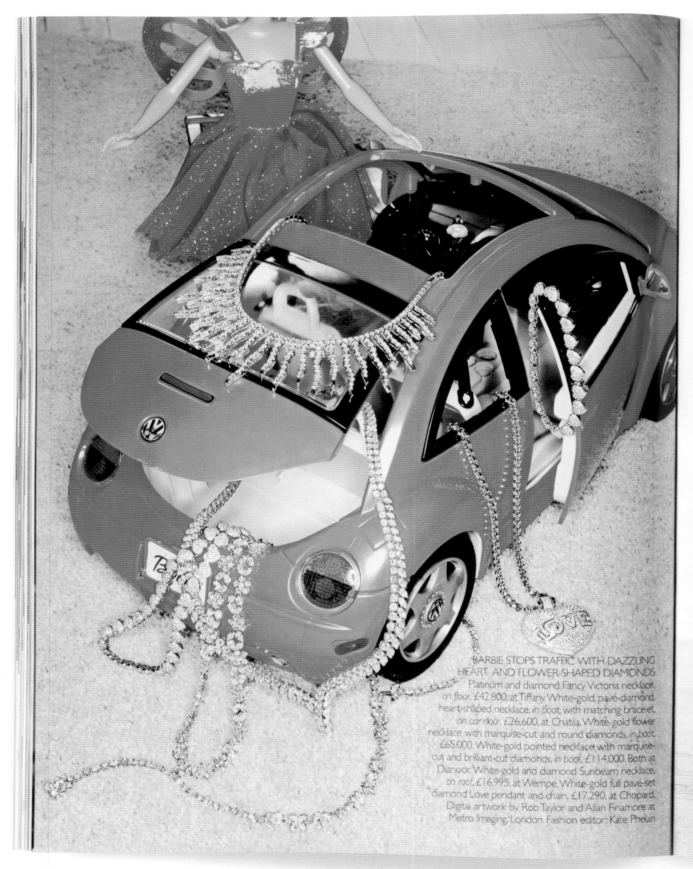

BARBIE STOPS TRAFFIC WITH DAZZLING
HEART- AND FLOWER-SHAPED DIAMONDS
Platinum and diamond, Fancy Victoria necklace,
on floor, £42,800, at Tiffany. White-gold, pavé-diamond,
heart-shaped necklace, in Boot, with matching bracelet,
on car door, £26,600, at Chatila. White-gold flower
necklace with marquise-cut and round diamonds, in boot,
£65,000. White-gold pointed necklace with marquise-
cut and brilliant-cut diamonds, in boot, £114,000. Both at
Dianoor. White-gold and diamond Sunbeam necklace,
on roof, £16,995, at Wempe. White-gold full pavé-set
diamond Love pendant and chain, £17,290, at Chopard.
Digital artwork by Rob Taylor and Allan Finamore at
Metro Imaging, London. Fashion editor: Kate Phelan

Vogue, July 2001, Great Britain

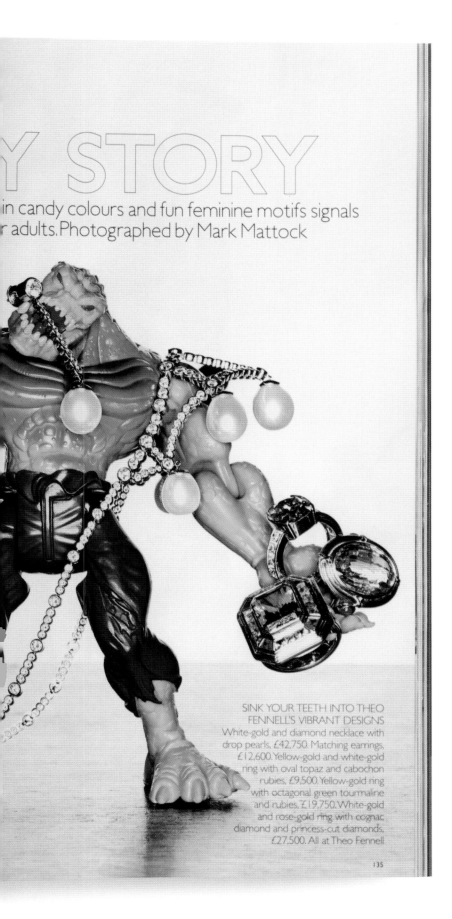

Y STORY

in candy colours and fun feminine motifs signals
adults. Photographed by Mark Mattock

SINK YOUR TEETH INTO THEO
FENNELL'S VIBRANT DESIGNS
White-gold and diamond necklace with
drop pearls, £42,750. Matching earrings,
£12,600. Yellow-gold and white-gold
ring with oval topaz and cabochon
rubies, £9,500. Yellow-gold ring
with octagonal green tourmaline
and rubies, £19,750. White-gold
and rose-gold ring with cognac
diamond and princess-cut diamonds,
£27,500. All at Theo Fennell

135

For kids and grown-ups. Mark Mattock sets the scene with jewelry
and toys in English *Vogue*.

Surface, No. 15, 1998, USA

Harper's Bazaar, May 2002, USA

Vogue, February 2001, Italy

Surface, No. 29, 2001, USA

Biba, May 2002, Spain

Nylon, September 2000, USA

Vogue, March 2001, Italy

The Fader, No. 9, 2001, USA

Prada

Già... anni '90? I fiori della primavera-estate 2001 dicono di sì, anche se ieri era: ornamentalismo, flo-cage artigianale e oggi è: stiliz-zazione botanica, computer garde-ning... Nuova flower-hour, con i fu-turibili Edith Sitwell prints di Dries van Noten, il bloom boom grafico di Prada, Valentino, Louis Vuitton, ma anche, per contrasto, i fiori "dentel-le" di Alberta Ferretti...

Moschino Cheap & Chic

veil n1 a piece of more or less transparent material, used to conceal or protect a woman's face and head. 2 take the veil. To become a nun. 3 Also called velum. Bot. a membranous structure, esp. the thin layer of cells covering a young mushroom. [from Norman F veile, from L Vele, pl of velum a covering]. net n1 a device used to protect or enclose things or to trap animals. 2 a plan, strategy, etc.. intended to trap or ensnare:the wearer slipped through the net. 3 Tennis or badminton, etc. 3a strip of net that divides the playing area into two equal parts. 3b shot hits the net. 4 Inf. 5 Short for Internet. 6 another word for work (sense2). [OE net; rel. to Gothic nati. Du. net] mask n1 covering for the whole or a part of the face worn for easement, protection, disguise, etc. 2 a likeness of a face or st, either sculpted or moulded, such as a death mask. 3 an ge of a face worn by an actor, esp. in classical drama, in order mbolise a character. 4 Surgery sterile gauze covering for the a and mouth worn to minimise the spread of germs. 5 a ing in the form of a face or ahead, Used as an ornament. 6 a ce placed over the nose And mouth to facilitate or prevent lation of a gas. 7 Photog; a shield of paper, paint, etc., placed an area of unexposed photographic surface to stop light ng on it. 8 the face and head of an animal, such as a fox. 9 to conceal; disguise; to mask an odour. [C16: from It. chera, ult. From Ar. maskharah clown, from sakhira mockery]

Dutch, July/August 2001, Netherlands

Dutch, January 2001, Netherlands

Mixt(e), No. 9, 2000, France

Vogue, December 2000, Italy

'Thunderbirds'. Photo sequence by Alan Scrymgeour for *Dutch*.

'Salute' by Duane Michals. Photo sequence based on scenes from Emily Brontë's *Wuthering Heights* for *Mixt[e]*.

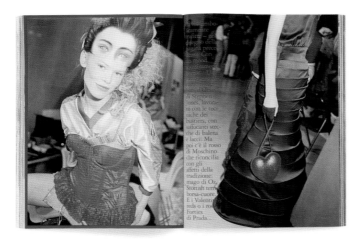

Photo sequence on red, the new trendy colour, by Anna Piaggi for Italian *Vogue*.

umkleide

MUT ZUM MUSTER
SCHÖN, WENN MODE EINEN BLEIBENDEN EINDRUCK HINTERLÄSST. SPUREN DER
AKTUELLEN KOLLEKTIONEN. *FOTOS: JOACHIM BALDAUF*

Süddeutsche Zeitung Magazin, No. 50, 2001, Germany

'Model Courage'. The models are wearing nothing but the marks left by their clothes.
Photographed by Joachim Baldauf for *Süddeutsche Zeitung Magazin*.

Selfservice, No. 14, 2001, France

Nylon, March 2000, USA

Top: Illustration by Julie Verhoven for *Selfservice*.

Bottom: Illustration by Tanya Ling for *Nylon*.

The Face, September 2000, Great Britain

Blvd., March 2001, Netherlands

Top: New Wave style in *The Face*. Styling by Simon Robbins, photographed by Sølve Sundsbø.

Bottom: One letter is sprayed onto the dress, the rest of the message is set in the layout by the designer.
Concept by Netty Nanta, photographed by Joakim Blöström for *Blvd.*

Nova, January 2001, Great Britain

Photos: Andy Snow, Stencils: Bernie Reid, for *Nova*.

Vanidad, March 2002, Spain

Photos: David Dunan for *Vanidad*.

Quest, Autumn 2001, Germany

Illustration: Alexander Gnädiger for *Quest*.

Vogue, No. 2, 2000, Italy

Current fashions in fur: different designers display drawings of their collections in Italian *Vogue*.

Deliciae Vitae, No. 1, 2001, Great Britain

You can hardly get closer – photo sequence by Robin Derrick for *Deliciae Vitae*.

Deliciae Vitae, No. 1, 2001, Great Britain

Deliciae Vitae, No. 1, 2001, Great Britain

Fashion show, computer generated by Faiyaz Jafri for *Deliciae Vitae*.

Likewise for *Deliciae Vitae*, this time illustrated by Jasper Godall.

Deliciae Vitae, No. 1, 2001, Great Britain

'Lover'. Photo sequence by Matthias Vriens for *Deliciae Vitae*.

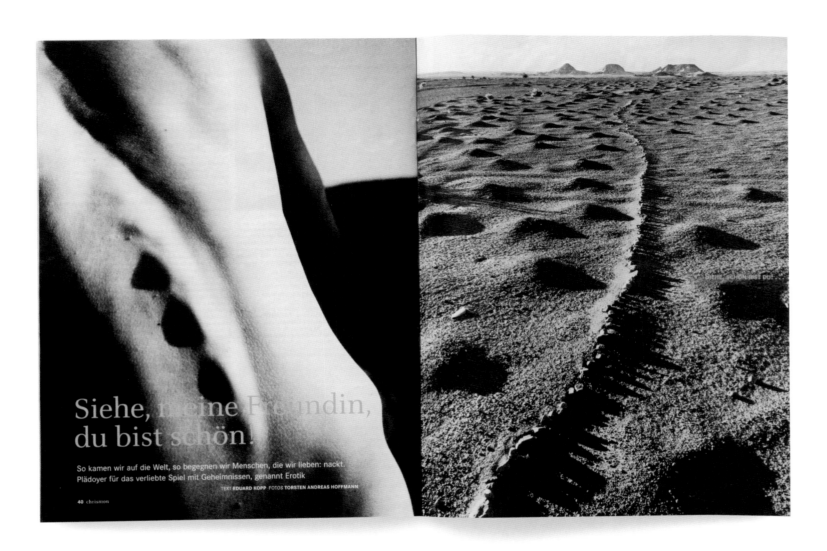

Siehe, meine Freundin, du bist schön!

So kamen wir auf die Welt, so begegnen wir Menschen, die wir lieben: nackt.
Plädoyer für das verliebte Spiel mit Geheimnissen, genannt Erotik

TEXT EDUARD KOPP FOTOS TORSTEN ANDREAS HOFFMANN

40 chrismon

Chrismon, August 2001, Germany

The human body and its counterpart in nature:
Thorsten Andreas Hoffmann for *Chrismon*.

NU
Jonvelle

«Une femme qui se sent
belle est la plus belle femme
du monde !» disait-il
et devant son objectif
le miracle s'accomplissait

«Je me sens photographe par passion et je ressens plus spécialement une passion irrésistible pour la femme...» «Je suis de plus en plus amoureux» disait-il. «Femmes, je vous aime» aurait-il pu chanter avec Julien Clerc.

Avec la photographie de nu, qu'il ne faisait qu'en noir et blanc, Jonvelle nous montre l'intimité, l'intérêt des femmes, ou plutôt, il en capte les moments fugitifs, les gestes, les attitudes. Le charme qu'ils déploient, même à leur insu, pour séduire les hommes, bien sûr, à a besoin de leur complicité pour duire le engagent de la séduction. Comme il fonctionnait à l'instinct, et qu'il aimait le rire, il faisait le père sans arrêt. C'était sa façon de mettre à l'aise les filles qu'il allait photographier mais les gens en général aussi, parce qu'il aimait les gens, il aimait la vie. Autant d'hommes que de femmes ont adoré son premier livre «Celles que j'aime». Les femmes ne révélaient que d'être prises en photo par lui, elles savaient qu'il les aurait rendues belles et sexy. Quant aux hommes, ils réalisaient tout d'un coup que leur petite amie pouvait être sublime alors qu'a priori elles n'avaient rien d'un mannequin justement.

Bernard Chapuis, l'un de ses amis, journaliste, a écrit comme introduction de ce livre épuisé sorti aux éditions Filipacchi en 1983 : «A demi vêtues d'un t-shirt, d'une culotte, de chaussettes, de draps de lit, de chaussures, d'une serviette sur la tête...

On imagine chacune de ces femmes marchant dans la rue, sortant du métro, descendant d'un taxi, achetant des cigarettes au tabac, écoutant les nouvelles à la radio. » Il nous fait vivre l'érotisme au quotidien. Sans maquillage outrancier, ni galet robes de princesse.

Ses photos de nus ressemblent à ses photos de mode, ou plutôt, il traite la mode comme le nu, car ce sont toujours ces gestes, ces attitudes naturelles qui comptent pour lui, plus que les poses. Il préférait ne pas travailler avec des mannequins professionnels qui à ses yeux avaient perdu toute spontanéité. Quand il ne pouvait pas faire autrement, il devait leur dire tout ce qu'il attendait d'elles, parce qu'elles ont totalement oublié ce qu'il voulait dire. Bien qu'elles soient nues, les femmes qu'il a photographiées, sont restées pudiques, il n'y a jamais là voyeurisme, ni indécence. «Ce que j'aime chez une femme, ce n'est pas tant ses charmes que son charme» disait-il. «La femme représente mon travail et ma vie.» Jonvelle était trop amoureux et respectueux des femmes. Il avait besoin de leur complicité pour les rendre belles. Et il savait les rendre belles, désirables même, car il savait qu'une femme qui se sent belle est vraiment la plus belle du monde.» Alors Jean-François Jonvelle faisait tout pour arriver à cela, et il parvenait plutôt bien. Il charmait à sa façon, en les faisant rire, bien sûr !

SERGE MOATTI
Son ami

A ses yeux, il savait donner son cœur. Dans ses photos, il savait mettre son âme. Sous son regard, les femmes se sentaient plus courageuse, les femmes plus belles. Un photographe de génie nous a suffied, Jean-François, nous a plusieurs tous.

ALAIN PANCRAZI
Producteur

Lors d'une soirée complice, Jean-François m'a confié un secret. Lorsqu'il aimera pour le grand voyage, il en profitera pour compter les étoiles. Et quand il aura toutes comptées, il reviendra parmi nous. Dépêche-toi, Jean-François, on n'attend.

DIDIER POUPARD
Son agent

Lorsqu'il y a deux ans, Jean-François Jonvelle entra dans mon bureau, je connaissais l'artiste mais c'est l'homme que je découvris au fil des jours. Son extrême gentillesse, sa grande disponibilité et son charme se faisaient un intérêt au travail. Aussi son absence s'en ressent-elle d'autant plus, maintenant qu'il n'est plus là.

PASCAL BRIARD
Ami et Directeur du marketing chez Canon

La passion de l'image avait accidentel nos rencontre un jour de l'année 1991. Par le suite, la fidélité, la générosité et si simplicité qui caractérisent la personnalité de Jean-François n'auront jamais cessé de conserver les fondations d'une très profonde amitié. Si Jean-François était «fou d'elles», il appartenait pour lui par à la grande famille de ceux qui étaient «fous de l'homme» et de son immense talent. Il me manque terriblement.

PATRICK DEMARCHELIER
Photographe

Jonvelle, c'est mes débuts de photographe, et il y prime toujours avec plaisir. C'était notre jardin des modes à nous avec tout ce que ça comporte comme souvenirs délectables et indélébiles, bien plus forts que la mort. C'était un photographe de talent.

Que ce soit le lavabo, le bidet, l'évier, le divan ou le réfrigérateur, c'est dans l'environnement familier que Jonvelle crée la surprise érotique.

Photo, March 2002, France
Jean-François Jonvelle for *Photo*.

BENOÎT DEVARRIEUX
Coprésident de l'agence DevarrieuxVillaret

CATHERINE BERGAUD
Une amie

PUBLIMOD' PHOTO
Son laboratoire

ALBANE NAVIZET
Photographe

MARYLINE BELLIEUD-VIGOUROUX
Directrice du musée de la mode à Marseille

ANDRÉ CARARA
Photographe

FRÉDÉRIC BEIGBEDER
Journaliste, écrivain et ami

BRUNO SUTER
Publicitaire

Wellfit, March 2001, Germany

SLOWER THAN A JAZZ BASS THOUGHTS UNWIND THIS LAZY BEAT

PUUR

fotografie Edel Verzijl @NRL | styling Caroline Fuchs @House of Orange | make-up Sil @House of Orange | modellen Kim Vos @Paparazzi, Rieka @Name Models, Ditta @Paparazzi, Eline & Carli Wassenaar | gedichten Written words: c Wonder | met dank aan Magic Mindz (locatie). Nieuw adres: Prins Hendrik kade 20-21 | font: Antoine

AND YES IT FEELS PERFECT TO BE DRESSED AS ME

Blvd., March 2001, Netherlands

Collezioni Edge, Spring 2002, Italy

Nova, September 2000, Great Britain

Citizen K, Summer 2000, France

Style, March 2001, Germany

The Face, July 2001, Great Britain

Vanity Fair, May 2002, USA

A very different view of make-up:
photographed by Tobias Zarius for *Style*.

'Hot mouths for hot nights'.
Lipstick as seen by Miles Aldridge for *The Face*.

Perfume underwater:
arranged by Susan Irvine and Gavin Shaw for *Vanity Fair*.

COAST 2 COAST

From the streets to your feets, local heroes demonstrate the look.

D.C.

Maybe all that sock gives a nice backdrop to D.C.'s famed "devastating dribble," 'cause if you don't have D.C.'s two crossover moves, you don't take the court. There's the below the knee, below the curb crossover—where only your shoes see your moves, shoes like these Nike Diamond Turf (above left). And then there's the high dribble, almost over the shoulder crossover. Local heroes Tyjuan Campbell, 14, Chris Turner, 14, Greg Lomax, 13, and Harris Hill, 14 mastered the moves on the hard streets, and if you don't believe it, try 'em.

In Washington D.C., where the big men roam at nearby Georgetown, they wear long socks, 'cause they're supposed to make you look taller. D.C. players copped it from notable area players Walt Williams, now of the Sacramento Kings, and Sherman Douglas, now of the Celtics. There are variations: Williams takes the sock almost over the knee; Douglas wears it three quarter, covering most of his calf. Lawrence Moten of Syracuse and Jerry Stackhouse of North Carolina are leading the way in the NCAA. And black sneakers, like these Nike Air Solo Flights (left) well, you gotta look bad in Bullet-town, USA.

N.Y.C.

In New York City, the shorts are baggy, the socks are low and the ethic is work, work, work. You won't find flashy T-shirts here, old tourney shirts are worn like badges of honor. Which they are, 'cause in New Jack City, they save the flashy stuff for the move to the hoop. If you can't take it strong to the hoop, you take it somewhere else. Here at the Gauchos gym in Da Bronx, Chitunder Weeks, 14, Vohn Hunter 14, Ernest Brown, 14 (yes, boys and girls, Junior is 6' 8"), Sirah Turner, 12, and Wakim Banks, 13, show that the only style is studying the game.

Parish DeBerry, 12, has a move or two of his own, zipping the ball between his Reebok Above the Rim's (below right). And those Nike Haurache's belong to Marcus Ferrer, 12. And they're black 'cause they're beautiful.

Crunch, Winter/Spring 2002, USA

Snow, No. 2, 2002, Germany

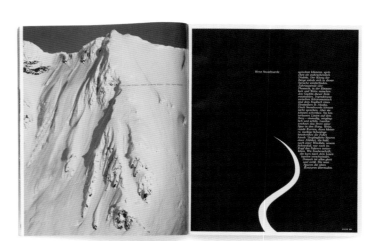

'Lines' by Arcu Sedwag, Jancsi Hadiç and Bertrand Boone
with text by Vera Schröder for *Snow*.

Snow, No. 2, 2001, Germany

Photo sequence on snowboarding in a 'new dimension' – photographed by Richard Walsh in 3D for *Snow*; the requisite glasses were also provided.

Wired, April 2002, USA

1/4 nach 5, March 2002, Germany

Line, Spring/Summer 2001, Great Britain

Report on kite surfing in Hawaii –
photographed by Stephen C. Whitesell for *Wired*.

The youth team of FC St Pauli –
portraits by Stefan Schmid for *1/4 nach 5*.

Sporting fashion – staged on the beach in Rio
by photographer Sesse Lind for *Line*.

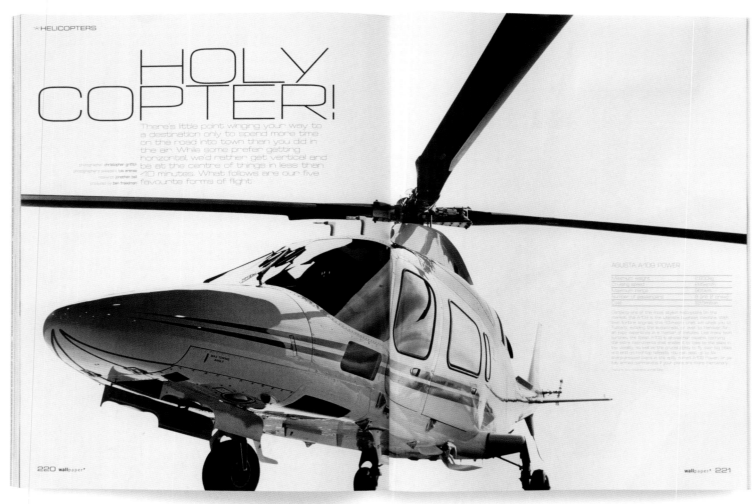

Wallpaper, May 2000, Great Britain

Dynamically staged: international helicopters,
photographed by Christopher Griffith for *Wallpaper*.

Below: Report on the Jaguar company.
Photos by Wilbert Weigend for *Premium*.

Right : The new Mini in Kapstadt.
Photos by Edgar Rodtmann, car illlustration
by Mustafa Malika for *Mini International*.

Middle and bottom right: BMW design study.
Photos by Simon Puschmann for *BMW Magazin*.

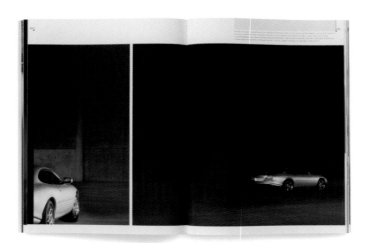

Premium, No. 1, 2001, Germany

Mini International, No. 1, 2002, Germany

BMW Magazin, No. 1, 2002, Germany

Mac Magazin, No. 3, 2000, Germany

'Like print'. Report on Xerox's 'electronic paper' in *Mac Magazin*.
Illustration: Boogie Entertainment.

Fast Company, No. 3, 2000, USA

'Information as if understanding mattered'. Report in *Fast Company* on Richard Saul Wurmans'
book *Understanding USA*.
Illustrations from the same book by Michael Donovan and Nancye Green.

Red Herring, No. 10, 2000, Great Britain

'Seoul Salvation'. Photo sequence by Graham Uden for *Red Herring*
on the production of microchips.

HP Omnibook, No. 3, 2001, Germany

Report on the company Echtzeit Ltd.
Maurice Weiss/Ostkreuz for *HP Omnibook Ready, Steady, GO!*

Right: 'Attack from Cyberspace'.
Illustration by 'Linientreu' for *Cine Chart*.

Cine Chart, No. 12, 2001, Germany

'Growing Pains'. Portrait
of the American firm THQ
for *Fast Company*.
Photos: David Tsay.

Fast Company, No. 10, 2000, USA

Fast Company, No. 9, 2001, USA

The bubble has burst. Report on the New Economy.
Photos: Len Irish for *Fast Company*.

'A star is born'. Report on the Euro.
Illustration: Michalke/Zaribaf for *Anleger*.

Anleger, No. 3, 2001, Germany

Brand eins, No. 3, 2002, Germany

Fast Company, No. 1, 2001, USA

Quote, No. 3, 1998, Netherlands

'People – Worlds'.
Photos by Janin Stötzner of people in the Altai Mountains in *Brand eins*.

'Man with a (talent) plan'.
Photographed by Debra McClinton of 'Electronic Arts' for *Fast Company*.

'De Pietje Bell bank'.
Photos: Bert Teunissen for *Quote*.

Süddeutsche Zeitung Magazin, November 1992, Germany

'Sex Murder'. Picture cycle by Jenny Holzer for *Süddeutsche Zeitung Magazin*.

DAE, 2001, Great Britain

Photos by Peter Morton and text by Gly Davis Marshall for *DAE*.

Baby, 2001, Netherlands

'Fashion Atlas of Anatomy'. Photographed by Koen Hanser for *Baby*.

Domus, July/August 2000, Italy

'Objects and concepts design' by Marti Guixé, photographed by Inga Knölke, accompanying text by Juli Capella.

Artbyte, September/October 2001, USA

'Aural surgeons'. Report on the Californian sound specialists 'Matmos' who, among other things, incorporate hospital sounds into their music. Photos: Tim Knox for Artbyte.

Baby, Spring 2002, Netherlands

'One minute sculptures' by Erwin Wurm, photos by Galerie Krinzinger, Vienna, text by Sharifa Jamaldin.

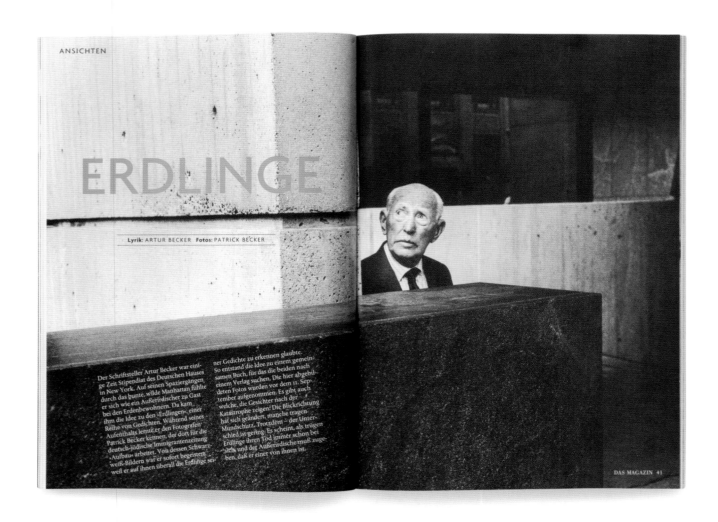

ANSICHTEN

ERDLINGE

Lyrik: ARTUR BECKER Fotos: PATRICK BECKER

Der Schriftsteller Artur Becker war einige Zeit Stipendiat des Deutschen Hauses in New York. Auf seinen Spaziergängen durch das bunte, wilde Manhattan fühlte er sich wie ein Außerirdischer zu Gast bei den Erdenbewohnern. Da kam ihm die Idee zu den ›Erdlingen‹, einer Reihe von Gedichten. Während seines Aufenthalts lernte er den Fotografen Patrick Becker kennen, der dort für die deutsch-jüdische Immigrantenzeitung ›Aufbau‹ arbeitet. Von dessen Schwarz-weiß-Bildern war er sofort begeistert, weil er auf ihnen überall die Erdlinge sei-

ner Gedichte zu erkennen glaubte. So entstand die Idee zu einem gemeinsamen Buch, für das die beiden nach einem Verlag suchen. Die hier abgebildeten Fotos wurden vor dem 11. September aufgenommen. Es gibt auch welche, die Gesichter nach der Katastrophe zeigen: Die Blickrichtung hat sich geändert, manche tragen Mundschutz. Trotzdem – der Unterschied ist gering. Es scheint, als trügen Erdlinge ihren Tod immer schon bei sich und der Außerirdische muß zugeben, daß er einer von ihnen ist.

DAS MAGAZIN 41

Das Magazin, March 2002, Germany

'Earthlings'. Interplay of pictures and poems in *Das Magazin – Die Lust zu lesen*.
Lyric poetry: Artur Becker. Photos: Patrick Becker.

Von Johann Wolfgang Goethe

une pièce pour ceux qui s'aiment

il est de nouveau là!

STELLA Es ist deine Stimme,
deine lebende Stimme! – 'Stella!
Stella!' – Du weißt, wie gern ich dich
deinen Namen aussprechen hörte:
'Stella!' Es spricht ihn niemand aus
wie du. Ganz die Seele der Liebe in dem
Klang! – Wie lebhaft ist mir noch die
Erinnerung des Tags, da ich dich ihn
zuerst aussprechen hörte, da all mein
Glück in dir begann!

stella

Soda, No. 17, 2001, Switzerland
Goethe meets candy colours – 'Stella' staged by Yoki van de Cream for *Soda*.

Slam Poetry transposed into
pictures by Neil Menussi and
Michael Levy for *Skim.com*.

Skim.com, No. 2, 2000, Switzerland

Süddeutsche Zeitung Magazin, No. 40, 2001, Germany

Little appetizers – individual pages from newly published books to start you reading. Photos: André Mühling for *Süddeutsche Zeitung Magazin*.

Brand eins, No. 6, 2001, Germany

'Short Sight, Long Sight'. A documentary on life, home and work in three continents for *Brand eins*.
Photos: USA, Imke Loss (top); Asia, Jan Siefke (bottom).

ADAC Reisemagazin, May/June 2001, Germany

'Faces of a Region'. Report on Southern Italy.
Ralf Kreuels for *ADAC Reisemagazin*.

Madison, No. 1, 2000, USA

Report on Inner Mongolia for *Madison*, with text by Anthony Smith
and photos by Gerald Foster.

Top: 'Tradition'. Illustration by François Berthoud for *Big*.

Bottom: 'In Search of Lost Time'. Travel report on the Mexican highlands with photos by Klaus Schoenwiese for *BMW Magazin*.

Big, No. 33, 2000, USA

BMW Magazin, No. 1, 2002, Germany

Blond, No. 3, 2002, Germany

Blvd., No. 4, 2001, Netherlands

Top: Report on a different kind of Japan in *Blond*, with illustrations by Imme Böhme and text by Gregor Wildermann.

Bottom: Declaration of love for Holland in *Blvd* with photos by Paul D. Scott and text by Lucas Mei.

NOTIONS OF NATURE

Bloom, December 2000, France
Inside pages 'Notions of nature'. Photos by Julie Chloe Degueidre.

Gardens Illustrated, December 2001, Great Britain

Martha Stewart Living, March 2001, USA

Martha Stewart Living, March 2000, USA

Martha Stewart Living, March 2000, USA

Martha Stewart Living, February 2002, USA

Eden, January 1999, Germany

Industrial Units. Photos by
Frank Breuer, awarded the Peter
Keetman Volkswagen Art
Foundation Prize for Industrial
Photography, reproduced in
Brand eins.

Brand eins, No. 3, 2002, Germany

Audi Magazin, No. 1, 2002, Germany

'Temples of the Modern Age'.
Report on football stadiums.
Photos: Bongartz/imago for
Audi Magazin.

Stockholm New, No. 12, 2002, Sweden

'Stockholm stone city'.Photos: Åke E, Son Lindman for *Stockholm New*.

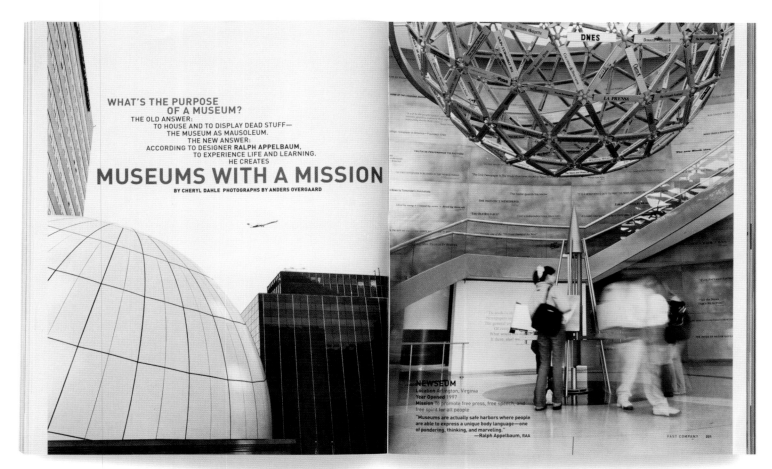

Fast Company, May 2000, USA

'Museums with a mission'. Photos: Anders Overgaard for *Fast Company*.

**CORNING MUSEUM
OF GLASS**
Location Corning, New York
Year Opened 1951 **Renovated** 1997–2000
Mission To engage, educate, and inspire
visitors and the community through the
art, history, and science of glass.

"We've rewritten the script for the Hot
Glass Show dozens of times, each time
adding more detail and information in
response to visitors' questions."
—Rob Cassetti, Corning Museum

Casa Vogue, December 2001, Italy

Brand eins, No. 3, 2001, Germany

Maison Française, May/June 2001, France

Visualizing medieval buildings through modern pop-up pictures.
Photos: Don Cunningham for *Casa Vogue*.

Photography and illustration combine to produce new realities.
Photos: Hartmut Nägele,
Illustration: Yves Netzhammer for *Brand eins*.

Report on 'Future Systems' furniture by Amanda Levete and Jan Kaplicky
for *Maison Française*. Photos: Richard Davies.

Room, No. 2, 2002, Germany

Wallpaper, March 2000, Great Britain

Stockholm New, No. 11, 2001, Sweden

Madison, January/February 2000, USA

Martha Stewart Living, January 2001, USA

Wallpaper, December 2000, Great Britain

AD, April/May 2002, Germany

Pom-Pom animals

Martha Stewart Living, April 2000, USA

HOW TO MAKE A BLUE JAY
Make two wool and mohair pom-poms: one large, the other small. 1. Wrap large templates with one-third white and two-thirds blue wool; add black wool in the center of one side. For the small ball, use half blue, half white wool. 2. Trim the large ball closer on the back than on the breast, making a plump oval. Have black and blue felt ready for the tail and beak. 3. Sew the pieces together. 4. Cut 8½ inches of black cloth-covered wire (30 gauge); fold so that one side is about ¾ inch longer. Crimp the wire into an approximate "M" shape as shown. Use needle-nose pliers to twist the three front claws into shape. Now shape that extra length of wire into bare foot. Twist the remaining wire tightly for strong legs. 5. Cut two triangles of black felt for the beak and a notched banner of blue felt for the tail. Attach them to the body with white craft glue. Put a needle threaded with knotted black cord though the small pom-pom to make eyes.

Perched on branches of flowering quince, this pageant of pom-pom BIRDS can be used as a springtime centerpiece. Add new species to the mix, and make enough twigs so that each guest can take one home.

241

OPPOSITE: Loopy white yarn best captures the curly wool of the LAMB. Make his long face stand out by closely trimming the wool on the front of the face pom-pom. The legs are felt-covered pipe cleaners, adhered with craft glue. THIS PAGE: This humble CATERPILLAR provides as much fascination as a creeper based on the stem of a sunflower. Yours doesn't have to be green; some caterpillars are brightly colored—orange, yellow, and black, for instance—to ward off hungry birds.

CREATED BY CLAUDIA BRUNO, MEGAN LEE, AND LAURA NORMANDIN

242   243

lifestyle

ES IST NOCH SUPPE DA!

GEMEINSAM ETWAS LECKERES KOCHEN SORGT GLEICH FÜR GUTE PARTYLAUNE. LASSEN SIE SICH VON FRANK BUCHHOLZ INSPIRIEREN

lifestyle

DS, No. 10, 2001, France

Room, No. 4, 2001, Germany

Big, No. 29, 2000, USA

Martha Stewart Living, February 2002, USA

Elle Bistro, February 2002, Germany

Wallpaper, June 2000, Great Britain

Wallpaper, January 2001, Great Britain

Big, No. 37, 2001, USA

Martha Stewart Living, March 2000, USA

Quest, February 2001, Germany

Marathonman

Quote, June 2000, Netherlands

Gwen Stefani and Terry Hall –
staged by Lizzi Finn (Artwork) for *Dazed & Confused*.

Dazed & Confused, No. 89, 2002, Great Britain,

Lenny Kravitz –
cool and simple by Christopher Witkin for *Surface*.

Surface, No. 15, 1998, USA

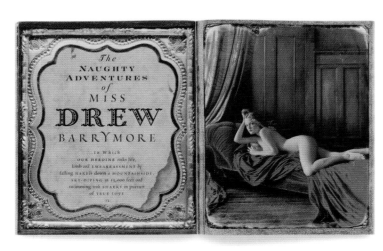

Drew Barrymore –
as seen by Mark Seliger for *Rolling Stone*.

Rolling Stone, November 2000, USA

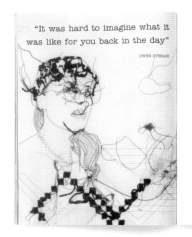

"It was hard to imagine what it
was like for you back in the day"

GWEN STEFANI

"We wanted to change the
world... but it was too big"

TERRY HALL

CHRIS HEATH

TO MARK the new millennium,
Drew Barrymore went to a
small Hawaiian island with
friends. At midnight, after
cooking food on a secluded beach, they
privately wrote down the resolutions
they wished to make on pieces of paper,
which they then rolled up and set on fire.
They dug a hole in the sand, a few feet
above the waterline, and buried the ashes.

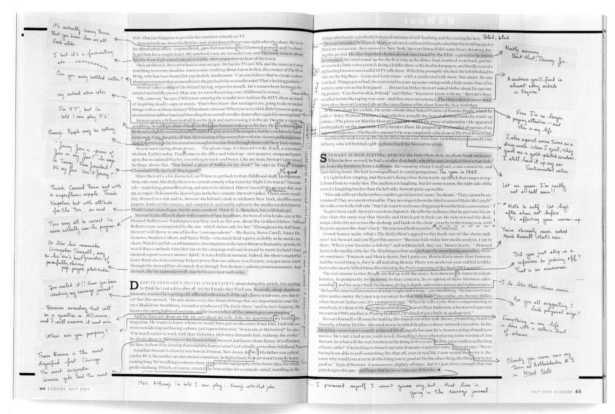

Esquire, No. 136, 2001, USA

Trace, No. 34, 2001, USA

Jalouse, No. 35, 2000, France

Life, No. 10, 1995, USA

Top: Report on a labour camp in Huntsville, Alabama. Photos: James Nachtwey for *Life*.
Right: 'A hole in the city'. Photos: Joel Meyerowitz for *The New Yorker*.

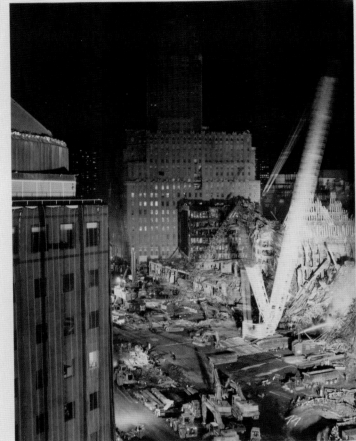

PORTFOLIO BY JOEL MEYEROWITZ

A HOLE IN THE CITY

Bordered on the north by Vesey Street, on the south by Liberty, on the east by Church, and on the west by West Street, the World Trade Center site comprises sixteen acres. Without the towers, it seems improbably small, as does the rest of lower Manhattan—shrunken somehow by disaster. The other day, two Spanish tourists who had come to see the site were questioning a police officer on duty nearby. They wanted to know where the second tower had been, and he tried to explain to them that it had been right there, right next to the first. "Dos edificios—no más," he said, gesturing at the empty space across the street.

Much of the area immediately surrounding the World Trade Center site has been reopened only in the past few months. "Please pardon our appearance during renovations," requests a placard posted in front of the Brooks Brothers that served as a morgue in the days after the attack. Some businesses have come back to the area—Starbucks, Century 21—but many have not. The words "NYPD Temp HQ—Med Trauma" are spray-painted in black and red on the windows of a defunct Burger King at the corner of Church and Liberty. On another empty storefront, "God Bless" has been scratched in the brownish-gray dust that still clings to most buildings in the area. Ten House, a fire station at the corner of Liberty and Greenwich Streets, was home to two companies, Engine 10 and Ladder 10. It lost four men, and is now being used as a command center for the recovery operations. "You must have an OSHA card for a respirator," a sign on the door reads. "No card, no resp. Got it?"

It was expected that the recovery and cleanup effort would take as long as a year. Instead, the job will be done in less than nine months. Some eight hundred people a day have been working in around-the-clock shifts, carting away more than a million and a half tons of concrete and steel. The statistics, grisly as they are, only hint at the magnitude of the horror. Workers have so far found more than nineteen thousand body parts. At this point, remains of less than half of the two thousand eight hundred and twenty-three victims have been identified.

Since the disaster, no one who is not directly involved in the recovery effort has been allowed on the site. For the most part, journalists were included in this ban, but, with the help of the Museum of the City of New York and sympathetic city officials, the photographer Joel Meyerowitz managed to obtain unlimited access. He has made more than a hundred visits, photographing "the pile," as the remains of the Trade Center came to be known, and the men and women working on it, at all times of the day and night. "Life took on a very different quality inside the zone," Meyerowitz says. "Even though you might have been doing ordinary things, they were being done in this pall of smoke and stench and fire and death." So far, he has taken more than seven thousand photographs; he expects to take a thousand more before he is done.

For those who want to get a glimpse of the site, the city has set up a viewing platform on Church Street. Every day, thousands line up, even though the view, at this point, is largely unremarkable: some gray construction trailers, men in white hard hats and fluorescent-orange vests, several American flags, and a deep hole in the ground out of which a truck occasionally rumbles. On a recent chilly weekday afternoon, the line stretched from Church Street down Fulton and around the corner onto Broadway, circling the graveyard behind St. Paul's Chapel. The graveyard fence was strewn with several generations of offerings—flags, flowers, stuffed animals, and T-shirts of rescue companies from around the country. As the crowd inched forward, the mood shifted. The chattering grew quieter, then stopped. Once up on the platform, people were allowed five minutes. They saw how little there was left to see, but remained, still looking for something. They took pictures, and then moved on.

—*Elizabeth Kolbert*

Panoramic view, looking northeast from the World Financial Center, across West Street to the World Trade Center site. September 25, 2001.

The New Yorker, May 2002, USA

Fast Company, No. 2, 2001, USA

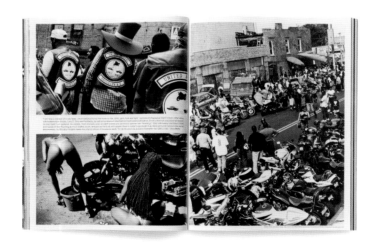

Dutch, March/April 2001, Netherlands

Top: 'Sweet Company' – Visit to Necco's. Photos: Michael McLaughlin for *Fast Company*.

Bottom: 'Chrome Cowboys' – Biker life in Brooklyn. Captured by Martin Dixon for *Dutch*.

Right: 'The world from my front porch'. Larry Towell shows his Ontario world in *Life*.

THE WORLD FROM MY FRONT PORCH

W HEN I was an adolescent, my father once scolded me for wanting to drive to Florida with a friend. It was too far from home, and I would be corrupted by the distance. I was 16. I'd been brought up on a small farm in Ontario and barely had been beyond 100 miles from home. Neither had he, at least not more than once or twice. He hated travel. He was rooted in the ground he stood on. The world for him was his front porch; it made him who he was.

Ten years after Ann and I were married, when we were expecting our third child, we bought a 75-acre farm at 40 percent of the owner's asking price. Its tiny small fields severed by roads, gulleys and a river, made it awkward for modern machinery, and much of the land was unproductive. Once I had my own front porch, however, I felt positioned in the world.

PHOTOGRAPHY AND TEXT BY
LARRY TOWELL

Ann holds Isaac on the front porch of their farmhouse in southern Ontario, as Moses looks on.

THE WORLD FROM MY FRONT PORCH

Most of these photographs were taken within 100 yards of the home. Although I travel extensively now, it is still with a sense of exile. From Hanoi to Managua, from San Salvador to East Jerusalem and the Occupied Territories, the longing for home persists. A photojournalist must work in the arena of international events. But when I am not traveling, I turn the camera inward.

Burying into a rural community demands an investigation of its history and a commitment to its past. One must treat the past as though it were the present. Many of my new neighbors could trace their ancestries to the first Scottish settlers of what was then Upper Canada. The front porch and original section of our house were built by pioneer surveyor Samuel Smith, who bought the farm in 1825 from the British Crown.

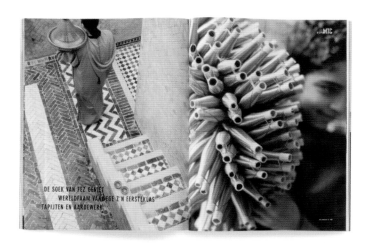

MTC, No. 1, 2001, Netherlands

Photo, No. 3, 2002, France

Mare, No. 18, 2000, Germany

Top: Morocco is green – as seen by Bernard Touillon for *MTC – More than classic*.

Middle: 'Vietnam Inc.' Philip Jones Griffiths for *Photo*.

Bottom: 'The Magic Sailors'. Report on the building of an East African dhow. Photos by Jack Picone, text by Alison Campell for *Mare*.

Max, December 1992, Germany

Max, November 1994, Germany

Top: Peter Lindbergh portfolio in *Max*.

Bottom: Richard Avedon portfolio in *Max*.

Matador, D, 1999, Spain

Peter Beard portfolio in *Matador*.

CLAUDE DITYVON

Dialoge mit der Nacht

Er zählt zu den wichtigen und zugleich immer
ein wenig verkannten Vertretern der französischen
Gegenwartsfotografie. Geläufig sind vor allem
seine atmosphärisch dichten Bilder vom
Pariser Mai '68. In seinem jüngsten Zyklus führt uns
Claude Dityvon durch das nächtliche Paris.

41

Leica World, No. 1, 2001, Germany

Claude Dityvon portfolio in *Leica World*.

SPINE DESIGN

Original magazine spines, and a design for the year

The binding of magazines varies according to the thickness. A thin one will be stapled through the spine, whereas thicker ones will be glued. The latter usually have a spine that's several millimetres wide, and many publishers like to fill it with the name, date and various themes of the magazine. But there are also designers who incorporate the spine into their design, either individually for each issue, or as a continuation throughout the year. In some magazines, there are even complete pictures or texts formed when all the issues of one year are placed together in the correct order. *Avenue*, a Dutch magazine, was one of the first to experiment with this idea, and it achieved some fine effects. Other magazines use the spine to display different colour codes. Which is the best direction for the text remains an open question; it really depends on how the magazine is likely to be stored – upright or lying flat – as well as on personal preferences.

Ad!dict, No. 15, No. 13, June 1998, No. 8, No. 10, Belgium

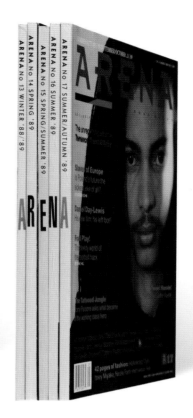

Arena, Winter 1988/1989, Spring 1989, Spring/Summer 1989, Summer 1989, Summer/Autumn 1989, Great Britain

Designers Digest, Nos. 65, 72, 70, 69, 76, Germany

Page, Nos. 1 – 12, 1997, Germany

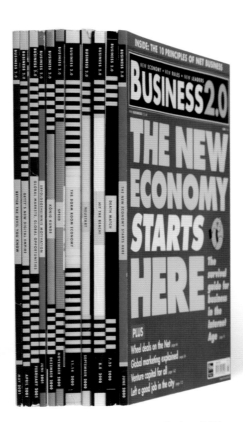

Business 2.0, February 2001, April – June 2001, June – September 2000, November – December 2000, Great Britain/Germany

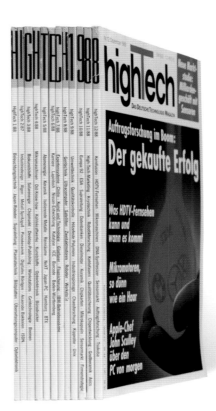

Hightech, Nos. 1 – 12, 1988, Germany

Brand eins, February – March 2000, October – November 1999, February 2001, June 2000, April 2001, October 2001, November 2000, May 2000, Germany

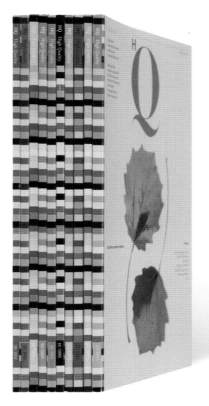

Spex, Nos. 1, 1999; 3 – 9, 1999; 11, 1999,
Germany

Wired, January 2000; January, April – June, November
2001; January – February 2002; May 2002, USA

High Quality, 20, 1991; 15, 1989; 12, 1988; 30, 199
19, 1991; 16, 1990; 26, 1993; 25 – 27, 1993, Germa

Avenue, January – December 1991, Netherlands

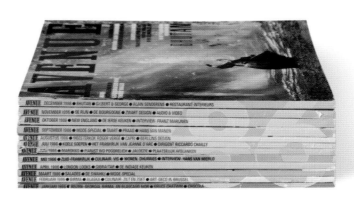

Avenue, January – December 1986, Netherlands

Avenue, January – December 1988, Netherlands

Avenue, January – December 1992, Netherlands

mare	Die Zeitschrift der Meere	No. 31	Sex
mare	Die Zeitschrift der Meere	No. 30	Pinguin
mare	Die Zeitschrift der Meere	No. 29	SOS
mare	Die Zeitschrift der Meere	No. 28	Zeit
mare	Die Zeitschrift der Meere	No. 27	Krebs & Krabbe
mare	Die Zeitschrift der Meere	No. 26	Kinder
mare	Die Zeitschrift der Meere	No. 24	Krieg & Frieden
mare	Die Zeitschrift der Meere	No. 23	Leuchtturm
mare	Die Zeitschrift der Meere	No. 22	Musik
mare	Die Zeitschrift der Meere	No. 21	Seepferdchen
mare	Die Zeitschrift der Meere	No. 19	Heilquelle Meer
mare	Die Zeitschrift der Meere	No. 18	Venedig
mare	Die Zeitschrift der Meere	No. 17	Essen & Trinken
mare	Die Zeitschrift der Meere	No. 16	Fliegen
mare	Die Zeitschrift der Meere	No. 15	Blau
mare	Die Zeitschrift der Meere	No. 14	Hai
mare	Die Zeitschrift der Meere	No. 13	Tiefsee
mare	Die Zeitschrift der Meere	No. 12	Hafen
mare	Die Zeitschrift der Meere	No. 10	Schweiz
mare	Die Zeitschrift der Meere	No. 9	Tintenfisch
mare	Die Zeitschrift der Meere	No. 8	Strand
mare	Die Zeitschrift der Meere	No. 7	Piraten & Meuterer

Mare, Nos. 7–10, 1998; Nos. 12–17, 1999; No. 19, 2000; Nos. 21–22, 2000; No. 24, 2001; Nos. 26–29, 2001; Nos. 30–31, 2002, Germany

Avenue, January–November 1984; June–December 1985, Netherlands

INDEX OF MAGAZINES

INDEX OF NAMES

Text by Ilse Moser and Horst Moser in collaboration with Stephanie Wiesner
Thanks to Stefanie Steiger

Translated from the German *Surprise Me* by David H. Wilson

First published in the United Kingdom in 2003 by Thames & Hudson Ltd,
181A High Holborn, London WC1V 7QX. Second edition published 2007.

This new edition revised and updated in 2011

Original edition © 2002, 2007, 2011 Verlag Hermann Schmidt Mainz and
Horst Moser

British Library Cataloguing-in-Publication Data
A catalogue record for this book is available from the British Library

ISBN: 978-0-500-51573-0

Printed and bound in China

To find out about all our publications, please visit **www.thamesandhudson.com**.
There you can subscribe to our e-newsletter, browse or download our current catalogue,
and buy any titles that are in print.